"I am so thankful that Cornelius Weaver has given practical and insightful attention to the important issues students face as they transition from high school to college. *Jesus Goes to College* addresses the challenges our students face and equips them for walking with Jesus as they transition to college."

—Linda Osborne,
Lifeway National College Ministry Leader

"*Jesus Goes to College* is a gift from God that will keep on giving. This book is a must for every high school graduating senior! It reminded me of the joy, hope, expectation, and even fear I encountered during my collegiate years."

—Pastor Gregory A. Wilson, Sr.
Living Water Church

"This young man has wisdom beyond his years!"

—Donna O. Johnson,
Guaranteed 4.0 Learning System

"I, too, have come to realize that only what you do for Christ will last. This is a great book for our time!"

—Pastor Vincent Hodge,
New Dimension Christian Ministries

JESUS

GOES TO

COLLEGE

JESUS
GOES TO
COLLEGE

CORNELIUS P. WEAVER

TATE PUBLISHING & Enterprises

Published by Tate Publishing & Enterprises, LLC
127 E. Trade Center Terrace | Mustang, Oklahoma 73064 USA
1.888.361.9473 | www.tatepublishing.com

Tate Publishing is committed to excellence in the publishing industry. The company reflects the philosophy established by the founders, based on Psalm 68:11,
"The Lord gave the word and great was the company of those who published it."

Book design copyright © 2011 by Tate Publishing, LLC. All rights reserved.
Cover design by Lauran Levy
Interior design by Lindsay B. Behrens

Published in the United States of America

ISBN: 978-1-61663-930-3
1. Education / Students & Student Life   2. Education / Higher
11.03.02

DEDICATION

To my loving family, thank you for your love and support.

In loving memory of my dad, Cornelius Weaver, who always knew that I would be a writer one day.

To my mother, Brenda Weaver, thank you for your patience and dealing with a busy son.

To my sister, Cydney Weaver, thank you for always laughing at my corny jokes.

To my beautiful and pleasant daughter, Noemie Eva Weaver; though college may be many years from now, I pray that these words will be your guide when you begin your collegiate journey.

To my pastor and first lady, Willie and Trina Kilpatrick, thank you for continued guidance and words of wisdom.

To my brother, Sheldon Shannon, thank you for being a brother born for the adversity in my life.

To my best friend, Monique Lucas, thank you for pushing me to finish, even when I had given up.

To my church family, Prince of Peace Missionary Baptist Church, thank you for nurturing my growth over the last decade of my life.

To the youth at Prince of Peace Missionary Baptist Church, I pray this will help you in your growth as young faithful believers.

To the students at Construction Careers Center Charter High School, I pray that this will inspire you to live a life for Christ.

To all my college classmates and friends that have joined me on this mission to follow Christ in college, may God continue to bless you and be with you.

TABLE OF CONTENTS

FOREWORD

It is very difficult to put together a thousand-piece jigsaw puzzle without that picture shown on the box. Yes, we all do better with a picture to illuminate our paths; without them, we stumble mercilessly and sometimes never finish.

We literally toss our dreams and hopes in the trashcan of despair out of pure frustration. Attempting goals and reaching heights without some visual clues to aid us with our journey makes life sometimes so difficult.

Jesus Goes to College is a wonderful flashlight to brighten the way for every high school senior and college freshman who has visions for success in their academic and spiritual lives.

This book gives great context clues on how to do it, how not to do it, and where to put it in college. Different kinds of burning questions are answered, even in areas that we all would like to keep under the cover.

Please study with great diligence your area of expertise, and in addition, make this book a part of your student curriculum and spiritual growth/development. Woven within these pages are rich lessons, stunning insights, and real-life applications.

—Willie E. Kilpatrick, Senior Pastor
Prince of Peace Missionary Baptist Church

INTRODUCTION

When I started college I knew that I needed a guide to help make the right decisions. I, like many of you, were filled with expectations and excitements, but also anxiety. I wondered how I would deal with the pressures of classes. *Should I go party? What friends would I have? How long will I be in school?* Faced with all of these questions, I looked to no one else but God for help. God assured me that all of my anticipation was normal for the stage and age that I was in life. He also enlightened my eyes to see practical insight in his Word to help me through this transition period in my life. *Jesus Goes to College* is a guide to making godly decisions as you transition to and walk through your college years.

So how did *Jesus Goes to College* actually come about? I was sitting on the edge of my bed in my dorm room my freshman year about two weeks into the semester. I was lonely, homesick, and I felt disconnected with everything around me. It was a feeling I had never felt before. The only item that was familiar in my life was the Word. I began searching through the Bible, and I discovered that Jesus had once been in the same position. He had already experienced every situation ahead of me, and there was no need for me to think that he did not know how I felt right now. "We don't have a priest who is out of touch with our reality. He's been through weakness and testing, experienced it all—all but the sin" (Hebrews 4:15, msg).

When God began to lead me to write about the story of *Jesus Goes to College,* he hadn't revealed to me that it would be a book. This was simply something for me in my daily reading. After freshman year, I had witnessed so many of my fellow classmates who proclaimed to know God begin to lose their integrity and values, and compromise so much of themselves due to bad decisions. Even I began to struggle to keep my faith in line in this different world. I began to ask God how could we have better prepared ourselves for college and the season ahead. Many time in my college years I sat down time and again trying to write this book, but it seemed I could never get anything going. It wasn't until God showed me in my last semester, that the reason I couldn't write the book then was because I had not experienced all of the college life I needed to live. I had to experience consequences of both good and bad decisions in order for my witness to be effective.

Now that I have graduated I can say that I made it through by faith in God, prayers of family and friends, and by the testimonies of other college students.

I encourage you to read every chapter within this book. Listen to what the Word of God is speaking to you in your heart, and then begin to make godly decisions in your college walk with Jesus.

—Cornelius W.

THE STORY OF
JESUS GOES TO COLLEGE

It's Time to Say Goodbye

> Every year his parents went to Jerusalem for the
> Feast of the Passover. When he was twelve years
> old, they went up to the Feast, according to the
> custom. After the Feast was over, while his parents
> were returning home, the boy Jesus stayed behind
> in Jerusalem, but they were unaware of it.
>
> Luke 2:41-43 (NIV)

The mile marker read six miles as we approached Rolla,
Missouri. I slept most of the way, trying my best not to
wake up through the hour-and-a-half drive. Between
the bumps of the highway and my anxiety, I woke up. I
looked over at my dad and noticed the twinkle in his eye
and the smile on his face as he proudly drove the car.

We arrived and unloaded both cars. My sister, brother,
and cousin had come to help out, so I moved in fairly

quickly. Before I knew it, my bed was made and my closet was filled with clothes.

After setting up my computer and packing my mini fridge with snacks, it was time to say our goodbyes. Mom continued to clean up, as if she didn't want the moment to come to an end. Dad looked around, complimented the room, and remarked that he thought this would be a good school for me. The moment finally came for us to part ways. For the first time in my life, I would be alone, away from my parents. Even though Rolla was only a little over one hundred miles away from home, it still felt like my parents would be on the other side of the world.

In my opinion, one of the hardest steps for parents is separating from their children. As children and students we have to understand our parents want to naturally hold on to their children. Our parents have now seen us go from diapers to diplomas. They have loved and protected us all of our lives. This transition is not only difficult for you but also for them. You may even notice your mom will begin to tear up or try to stay a little while longer in your new dorm room. This is a moment of transition. Don't rush through this moment.

Be sympathetic to your parents feelings in the separation phase. Often my friends and I have complained of how our parents continue to call us and text us (still trying to make sure that we made it in), checking up on us as though we were at home. I even remember witnessing a friend of mine tell her mom rudely, "You wouldn't know if I'm out or not, because you're not here!" Remember, the Word still calls us to "Honor our mother and father"

(Ephesians 6:10, KJV). Though this is a season of independence, it is not a season to be disrespectful or neglect home. Keep the lines of communication open. Make your parents feel appreciated with occasional calls and updates. Respect that they have contributed to your success. Let them know you have a purpose in this time of separation that has to be fulfilled.

There was a reason for Jesus separating from his earthly parents. God sent his Son, Jesus, to earth for a purpose, to fulfill a mission that only he could do. "The Spirit of the Lord is upon me, for he has appointed me to preach Good News to the poor. He has sent me to proclaim that captives will be released, that the blind will see, that the downtrodden will be freed from their oppressors" (Luke 4:18, NLT). Jesus not only recognized that he had purpose on his life, but separating from his folks was a step to begin to fulfill the purpose in his life.

In taking these steps, Jesus had to step out of tradition during his ministry. It was the custom to return home after the feast of the Passover. However, Jesus had a purpose to fulfill and decided to stay behind. No, Jesus did not stay behind to be disobedient to his earthly parents, Mary and Joseph, but Jesus decided to stay behind to be obedient to his heavenly parent—God.

From Scripture we know that he was astounding the doctors of the law, and from Judaic perspective, he was approaching the age of maturity when he would prove himself to be a student of the law. The significance of this event is that he was to the point where all that he had learned would be put to action. His knowledge of the law and the Word would be tested. This is your season to be proven and tested and to put all the values you learned at home to action.

In my opinion, certain life skills cannot be learned if you always have the comforts of home. Even when detaching from home, you may encounter some resistance. I have learned that people don't necessarily hold you down out of spite, envy, or even just plain hatred. Sometimes they hold you down out of fear of losing you. Just look at Peter. Here is Jesus, beginning to explain how he must go and suffer many things and must ultimately separate from the disciples. The disciples are like parents who don't want to let go. Peter said, "Never, Lord! This shall never happen to you." Peter didn't say it to be mean, but he did not want to lose the Jesus to whom he had grown so close to. Jesus replied, "Get behind me, Satan! You are a stumbling block to me; you do not have in mind the things of God, but the things of men" (Matthew 16:22-23, NIV). Now please don't go around calling your parents "Satan." That would not help you with getting extra pocket cash for school. However, recognize those who are like Peter, who did not have in the mind the broader vision of what God was going to accomplish. Separation is vital for you going into greatness as a college student. Time away from parents will develop responsibility and the necessary life skills to be successful. Accomplished students are those who learn to balance time and responsibilities well and greatly value their education.

Your Education Is Valuable

After three days they found him in the temple courts, sitting among the teachers, listening to them and asking them questions. Everyone who heard him was amazed at his understanding and his answers.

Luke 2:46-47 (NIV)

When I was in high school my father would always say, "An unorganized surrounding means an unorganized mind." Then he would go into his speech on the value of order and education. He emphasized over and over again about how much I needed to get organized with my schedule and take my education seriously. He had never gone to college and didn't finish high school either. Though my father had a lot of great success, he knew that he would have experienced fewer struggles in life if he had gotten a college education. One day I told myself that I would begin to start "redeeming the time" (Ephesians 5:16, NIV). *Redeem* means to get the value out of or extract from. If you have ever been to the store and looked at a coupon, normally it will say "redeem this coupon" by a specific date. This lets you know that after that date the coupon is no longer of any value. If you choose to be lazy, party, or sleep away your college life, it will soon become worthless. You have to redeem the time. Taking value in your education not only means redeeming the time but also having the right motive for being in college.

Today's generation, in my opinion, is motivated simply by a degree that will sit on our wall, but we miss the opportunity to learn more about an interest that we currently have. I asked a friend once when she was supposed to graduate and she sighed. "About a year from now." I asked why, and she said she changed her major.

When I questioned her again, she said, "I initially started to chase the money, but now I am chasing my passion." College is the place to chase your passion. It is the space to cultivate our thinking into a targeted area of architecture, music, education, engineering, business, or whatever your hopes may be until you have achieved it.

In fact, the degree itself only validates to corporate America and the outside world that you are a thinker. Thinkers accept the challenges of school and enjoy their major because it brings them fulfillment. Some of my classmates that I have met through college seemed unmotivated about school and their major. They simply came to college because their parents expected them to. They really didn't see any value in getting an education and only wanted to make their parents happy. There is nothing wrong with making your parents happy, but at the expense of your own happiness, it is wrong, and it may cause you great frustration later on in life.

Getting an education is the right thing to do. Yes, I know everyone cannot afford college, but there are other avenues of higher education. You can go to community college, technical school, cosmetology school, business school, and you can even get an online degree, but it is important to place yourself in an environment of progressively thinking people. You will only become educated when you surround yourself with educators.

We have to be thrilled to be in college and able to get an understanding of things our friends and parents could only dream of. One of my professors always said, "College gives you the learning and the opportunity to understand how you can change the world." Cherish the college experience of education and value that it will bring fulfillment to your purpose in college. Not only is understanding the value of your education great but accompanying that appreciation with an academic major will glorify God.

What's Your Major?

> And he said unto them, How is it that ye sought me? wist ye not that I must be about my Father's business?
>
> Luke 2:49 (KJV)

Now that you are in college and you understand the value of an education, what are you going to major in while at college? In my opinion, this is bigger question that the majority of college students lose sleep over. Many students spend most of their college life unsure of the direction in the courses they're taking.

I, on the other hand, was the oddball. When I was in the second grade, my teacher handed us the brown, thick-ruled paper and told us to write what we wanted to be. I wrote, "I want to be an archikect." (Yeah, I know I wasn't that great at spelling then.) Yet, God had already developed the desire in my heart. My desire developed through my hobbies of Lincoln Logs and breaking old videotapes by building houses with them. I even used to make these huge fortresses out of couch pillows in the basement and invite my friends over to crawl through them. Even then my interest was there for building and engineering.

Before we were born, God had a plan for our lives. It is up to us to develop the interest that he has put in our hearts. However, until we hear from God, we don't know how we should be used for God's kingdom and what ministry we should be involved in. God wants to take our interest and use them for his glory. I knew that being an engineer would be great for me because it was something I was attracted to and liked. It was only later as time went by that I knew it would be even greater for God's kingdom. Now I pray that God uses my profession to help build churches, community centers, and any facility that will edify his kingdom.

God has a say so in our careers. Remember it was Jesus who spotted Simon Peter trying to catch fish by the water's edge one day. Simon Peter was frustrated that he hadn't caught any fish all day. Jesus told him, "Put out into deep water, and let down the nets for a catch" (Luke 5:4, MSG). Peter then said, "Master we've worked hard all night and haven't caught anything. But because you say so, I will let down the nets" (Luke 5:5, MSG).

Peter was in the position where he should have caught some fish because he had been trying all day long, yet he hadn't.

Frustration happens after you find yourself in the position that produces no results. He hadn't caught one fish. You can be at the best school in the country, but it means nothing until you catch a fish. Catching fish is symbolic of being productive. During college you will become frustrated, and it will seem like you are non-productive, yet if you know that your major is God-given, it will help you stick with it.

After Peter had finally listened to Jesus, he saw the rewards because he now had a ton of fish. Peter was willing to give his life, his career, and all he had to be in line with Jesus.

Then Jesus spoke the following powerful words, "From now on you will be fishers of men." Jesus was basically saying, "I am going to combine your career and ministry in order to perform my will." Sometimes we try so hard to be something that we are not. We try out majors and think, *Maybe I can mold it to my liking,* or *maybe this will pay the most,* but then later realize that we would have saved time, energy, and tears if we had gone with what the Holy Spirit was telling us in the first place.

Jesus was sure of what he was doing at the temple because he was in God's will. He wasn't just there to be there; he was not simply going through college with no idea of self or purpose. When asked why he had left, he replied, "He was to be about his father's business." Jesus had a major purpose, so he declared a major decision, and that was to follow what God wanted him to do.

When you arrive on the college campus, before you enroll, before you go to the first party of the semester, begin to pray about your major. Under no circumstances should you declare just any major. Choosing a major that God didn't intend for you will have you fishing on the wrong side of the boat.

Importance of Graduation

> And Jesus increased in wisdom and stature, and in favor with God and man.
>
> Luke 2:5 (kjv)

It's graduation day, and you are the center of all family's joy, pride, and excitement. People shower you with praise, gifts, and most importantly, love. This day seems all worth it. Over the last four or five years, or however long it took you to graduate, you've thought about this one day. I can still remember. This is the day you were waiting for. Even with all those tests, long study hours, days when you didn't sleep enough, classes you had to drop and take over, it all seems to be worth it for this day.

Graduation is advancing from one level to the next. You have now made it to the next level in life. Walking across the stage brings excitement to your parents, hope to younger brother or sister, and maybe even life to that young person at your church who looked up to you.

Jesus advanced to the next level after leaving the temple and conversing with scholars. He had a higher level of thinking and increased wisdom; I'm not saying that he didn't already have wisdom, but what he had was increased to because Jesus engaged himself in that arena of education.

College is a ground for gaining. You will gain knowledge, maturity, and life skills that will assist you in your journey after college. Certain life skills like paying bills and money management are prayerfully learned while in college. Being able to fix yourself a hot meal without burning down the kitchen and cleaning up after yourself are basic life skills that you should have grasped while in college.

Most things that you will graduate from don't come with an announcement on stage. Most life skills learned in college will go unrecognized formally; however, they are essential for growth. I promise you there will be no degrees handed out for spiritual maturity, emotional stability, and financial acumen at graduation. Yet these are some of the most important aspects of life that should elevate in you.

Another part of graduation is favor with God. God now grants you another level of favor upon graduating. What does that mean? Before you were reaping blessings at the level of a college student, and now God has transitioned that favor so that you will be able to reap elevated blessings in the business world. At this time God may have already allowed you to receive a full-time job offer. God may have already poured out that huge salary that you were praying for. You are now operating on a whole new level, and many doors have been opened for you simply because you were obedient to God all those years in college by being in the place where you should have been. "Blessed is the man who finds wisdom and the man who gains understanding" (Proverbs 3:13, KJV). Jesus gained understanding when he added to his wisdom that day in the temple. You will too!

Class Notes:

- It's time to say goodbye— leaving home can be difficult, but can be done with purpose and respect for your parents.

- Your education is valuable—wanting to redeem the time in college and to cultivate your interests.

- What's your major? —combining your academic major with God's purpose in your life.

- Importance of graduation—graduation demonstrates that you have the life skills to be successful beyond college.

WHERE AM I GOING?

Choosing the right college should not be done without prayer and practical consideration. Prayer allows God to speak to your heart. God speaks in many forms. A few of them are: life circumstances, godly counsel, and the peace of God. Prayer will also keep you from developing the spirit of fear. Being afraid to apply to schools, wondering how to pay for college, or even being tempted to transfer schools are all natural fears. However, we know that, "...God hath not given us the spirit of fear; but of power, and of love, and of a sound mind" (2 Timothy 1:7, KJV). We need to stop operating in the natural fears and access God's supernatural power through prayer. This is the best time to start a prayer life, if you haven't already, because it is vital while making this life-changing decision.

> "Is there anyone here who, planning to build a new house, doesn't first sit down and figure the cost so you'll know if you can complete it? If you only get the foundation laid and then run out of money, you're going to look pretty foolish.

Everyone passing by will poke fun at you: 'He started something he couldn't finish'.

Luke 14:28-30 (MSG)

God Speaks through Circumstances

When you don't pray, you only see what you want. In my senior year of high school my football coach introduced me to a college recruiter who had seen a few of my games and was interested in having me play football. I politely listened and asked about the school and what they had to offer. More specifically, I asked if they had a program for architecture. He commented they had just started a program similar to that. It sounded okay, but it wasn't what I wanted. I wanted to go to Washington University. So without praying I applied to Washington University and didn't give the other school a second thought. Three months passed, a letter from Washington University came, and I opened with no hesitation. To my disappointment, it began, "We regret to inform you..." I stopped there because that's all I wanted to read. I was shocked and in tears. Yet at this same time a week before, the recruiter called me again and was awaiting my decision. I had delayed giving him a decision for three months. I was one of the last recruits to commit and also missed the deadline for the scholarship by a few days.

Closed doors will prevent you from moving forward in your own pursuits. There I was about to forfeit a blessing that was chasing after me because I was pursing a dream that was not for me. God had provided practical means for me to go to the school of his choice, but I didn't recognize it. Look where God is providing practical means to go to school. That's a clear sign that God is giving you the thumbs up. It may be through a scholarship, grant, or other sources of funding. We know our God to be Jehovah-jireh (Genesis 22:14, KJV), which means he is our provider. Provision to go to the college is one key to hearing his voice on your decision. God will not only speak through circumstances but through mature counselors in our lives as well.

God Speaks through Wise Counsel

Mature, godly counsels comes from those who have your best interest at heart. Your guidance counselor, teachers, and parents have years of wisdom to share with you. Many have been to college and can give insight on how to choose the right one. Even if you have a sense of what your right college is, their guidance can confirm what God is telling you.

Not listening to godly wisdom can cost you your future. In 1 Kings 12:1-19 (NIV), Rehoboam became the newly appointed king. He had to make a decision to either give the people some slack with respect to labor or become an even tougher leader than his father. Rehoboam consulted with his elders but ignored their wisdom and sided with those who were his own age. His decision to be an even tougher leader, ultimately caused the split of the kingdom and strife between the two nations. Choosing to listen to your friends over the advice of your parents, counselor, or teacher may have consequences that you will not like. Listen to those around you who have been where you are trying to get. They have a good idea of the challenges ahead.

Confirmation comes through two or three witnesses. The Lord has a way of sending people in our lives to serve as road signs to let us know we are going in the right direction. When I debated going to University of Missouri-Rolla (UMR), there were many people who told me they had graduated from there. Then, one of my mentors in the industry told me that it was the best school for my chosen career path. I respected him, and he was person of integrity and successful in his career. I knew that he had my best interest in mind with the advice he'd provided.

God Will Speak through Peace

Having the peace of God is the seal on your decision. After God has spoken through resources, wise counsel, and prayer, the peace of God seals the deal. Knowing you have God's peace is reassuring. It provides confidence that God has blessed your decision and that your future is in his hands. When you have the peace of God, you no longer think about the "what ifs" or the "maybe I should haves." His peace passes our own capacity and puts our mind at ease.

After I made my decision, I was at peace. The decision had been made and the pressure to decide was over. However, the peace didn't come from making the decision. The peace was a result of seeing God in my decision. Your peace will come when you see how God guides your decision to fit his will. However, once you find his peace and joy in your decision, be aware that the enemy will set out to try to take that from you.

Don't Be Afraid to Apply

Lack of prayer creates fear and diminished faith in God. Most of the time you keep yourself from the things that God would have for you because you do not think you can receive them. You discredit yourself and say that you're not smart enough, or that your ACT or SAT scores are not good enough, or maybe you just don't have enough money to afford it.

I remember a time in high school when our football team hadn't won a homecoming game in years. Having not won a homecoming game in years was considered a curse at our school. I also remember how we (the seniors) thought it would all change, yet in the back of our heads we kept thinking about the curse. That night we lost by one point; in fact, we lost by one yard—one yard away from breaking the curse. We could have lost by any amount of points that night, because from the beginning of that game we played scared. We made our opponents out to be something that they were not. Stop playing scared and making the college application/decision process out to be something it is not.

When Israel sent twelve spies out to survey Canaan, they searched the land. After returning, ten of the spies reported that although the land was full of milk and honey, it also had giants that make them look like grasshoppers in comparison. They were convinced that there were great things ahead, but they could never achieve them because of fear. Yet, there were two that came named Joshua and Caleb, and they said, "Let us go up at once, and possess it; for we are well able to overcome it" (Numbers 13:30, NKJV). Many of you will determine that the Ivy League schools, and the prestigious schools are great, but you will make yourself out to be a grasshoppers when applying to college. You will think that all of your achievements, scores, and stature are insignificant. If God has told you that you should go to that dream college, then you are well able and equipped to take the step. After you have listened to God and he has called you to a particular place, know that he has qualified you for it. When you know God has you in a certain place, even when worries arise you will not fall to the temptation to leave or quit.

If You Feel Tempted to Transfer

Prayer combined with reciting your initial reasons for your decision will help you in the face of challenges. Toward the end of my first year, I began to get frustrated with the strenuous demand of football, academics, and the fact that I was just wasn't enjoying small-town college life. I felt like all my other friends had gone to big colleges, and I didn't think anything else was going on in little Rolla, Missouri.

For spring break I visited a friend of mine in Atlanta. It was exciting to see a party college town in my eyes. I fell in love with that city. I was determined that I wanted to leave my small college town life. I thought the grass looked greener on the other side. I then began to make plans on how I would transfer. I started to make plans to get to Atlanta. Yet the Lord had not told me anything. It was a lot of my own efforts and not God's will.

It finally came down to April of my freshman year. I was doing a video promotion for the school on the importance of education and value of having a vision in college. The interviewer began to ask me questions on why I had come to this school. "How did I pick the college?" "What is important to me?"

As I began to give the answers subconsciously, I began to reaffirm why I was at this college opposed to any other college! I began to reaffirm my purpose and vision as to why I was here. After that interview, I knew where I belonged. Five years later, I knew it was God. Just through my experiences, my growth on that campus improved my life as a believer. Just think, if I had forced my way into Washington University or had transferred to Atlanta, I might not even be writing this book right now.

Class Notes:

1. Prayer will allow God to speak through circumstances.
2. Prayer will allow God to speak through wise counsel.
3. Prayer will allow God to speak through the peace of God.
4. Prayer will keep you from being fearful about applying to colleges.
5. Prayer will give you faith for God's provision.
6. Prayer will keep you from being tempted to transfer.

1. Have you prayed about where you should go for school? If so, have you noticed God speaking through circumstances, wise counsel, and the peace of God?

_____

_____

2. Are you afraid to apply to a college? Why are you afraid?

_____

_____

Prayer for determining your college:

Lord Jesus, I ask that you guide my decision in where you would have me to go for my education. I don't want to be swayed or confused by the opinions of others, but I want to hear from you. Show me how I am going to pay for school. Be clear in your voice so that I follow in the right path. You said that the steps of a good man are ordered by the Lord. Order my steps in this decision. Give me favor in every area on the application process, any scholarship, and even help me adjust but not compromise to the culture of the campus. Lead me. Guide me. In Jesus's name. Amen.

PENCIL, PAPER, AND PRAYER

Deciding to develop good study habits with a prayer life will lead to success in your classes. Prayer before you study will keep you from feeling inferior and open up understanding from God. Useful study skills will sharpen your ability to perform on tests. Being a concerned and involved student will gain you favor with your teachers. When you do all of these, you position yourself for future achievement in college.

Don't Be Fooled

Over the years, many of my friends have said, "I am not good at taking tests!" or "I understand it, but I just can't put it on paper." Some of us have even felt inferior to our other classmates at times. Some topics just seem to come easier to others and harder to some. It even frustrated me at times that I would spend more time studying than others but not get the grade I expected. If we are not careful, we can begin to become envious of others and their success. "But as for me, I came so close to the edge of the cliff! My feet were slipping, and I was almost gone. For I envied the proud when I saw them prosper despite their wickedness" (Psalm 73:1-3, NLT). David writes this to let us know he was about to fall out of his relationship with God all because he wanted something the wicked had. This is not saying all of your classmates who make good grades are wicked. It warns us against being envious of your other classmates, no matter what grade they get. You just keep your head up and continue to focus on God and know that he does not grade us the same way our professors grade us. God has designed you ever so unique. "You are fearfully and wonderfully made" (Psalm 139:14, KJV).

I remember one semester patiently waiting outside of Dr. Lewis's office, my academic advisor, as I had done the last four and a half years. I had my degree report in hand. I couldn't wait to have my last advisor meeting to plan my final semester class schedule.

We joked as always and conversed as we highlighted the remaining classes. As he printed out my copy, he asked, "Is there anything you would have done differently?" Now , mind you, if you looked over my transcript, you would have noticed that every letter of the alphabet was on there, from A to F and even an I and some symbols. I looked at all of that and then said to him, "I wouldn't change a thing," and I smiled.

The reason I said what I said in Dr. Lewis's office is because I knew that I received knowledge and understanding in all the subjects I had studied. "In all thy getting, get an understanding" (Proverbs 4:7, KJV). The Bible did not say, "Go get an A." It did not say, "Get the best grade." It said, "Get an understanding." This is not to say you shouldn't strive for excellence in your course work. Certainly, you should aim for the best. However, there is a rewarding feeling in both having an excellent grade and a true understanding of the subject.

As Jesus strayed into the temple he approached the scholars, he began to ask questions and receive answers. This season in college is yours to ask questions and receive those answers. Look at college as the wealth of knowledge at your fingertips, and you can obtain it all if you would just seek after it.

Learn How to Fail

Another vital component to apply to your success in this season of education is learning how to fail. I guess you say, "What do you mean learning how to fail?" Paul said, "...I have learned to be content whatever the circumstances" (Philippians 4:11, NIV). This really helped me to celebrate all of my college grades. Yet some of us never get a chance to celebrate God, even when we fail. God is not just in the As and Bs of life. He is in every letter grade. Once I was told that I would be dropped from a class because I was at a 66 percent and a 68 percent in the course was needed to continue. I was not even halfway through with the course. I was frustrated, disgusted, and upset at the teacher, myself, and God. Now that I look back, I am so glad I that I was forced to drop that class because it freed time up for me to plan the gospel concert that semester. The concert was done with the spirit of excellence. The concert displayed Christ's love through song, skit, and preaching the word. So many of my class-mates of mine were able to come to Christ. Just think: if I had not failed, someone would have never received our Lord and personal Savior, Jesus Christ. Learn how to fail, and you will quickly be educated on how to succeed in Christ. You never know what God wants to do with your failures. God is in control of your academics; however, we must study and apply good habits as well as trust God when we take our exams.

Taking the Test

Throughout college life, your grades are ultimately deter-mined by taking tests. Practical steps to better test grades would obviously be to study, review frequently, and ulti-mately perform under minimum pressure. On tests it seemed easy to forget things that you have so surely stud-ied, but I would always say, "But the Counselor, the Holy Spirit, whom the Father will send in my name, will teach you all things and will remind you of everything I have said to you" (John 14:26, NIV).

I have been in the middle of the test and literally blanked out with no idea of what I was doing. Then all of a sudden, God would allow it to come back to my memory. Not only during the test but also during the times of study and preparation for the test. I remember I was studying for a final that everyone was nervous about.

The final was supposed to be incredibly hard. Yet I said to myself, "Is there anything too hard for God?" So some friends and I studied the night before. We normally studied well pass midnight. It was around nine o'clock that God had told me exactly what to study. He pointed at the chapters, the concepts, and put me at peace. I started packing up, and no one knew why. I was leaving, and they thought that I would do terribly on the test because I had not studied enough. I could have explained that God told me exactly what would be on the test, but I doubt that they would have believed me. I left, took the test the next day, and to God's glory, got an A on it! God is good! Moreover, there is nothing too hard for our God. He not only positions you for peace on your tough test, but can give you favor with your teachers as well.

Favor with the Teacher

God wants us to acknowledge him in front of everyone and to not be ashamed. One thing that I started doing my second semester in school was to write "Jesus is Lord" above my name in the right-hand corner of my test papers. I never did it to be overly spiritual or a "super Christian," but I did so that whoever was grading the test would have to see that his name is above every name and that Jesus was first in my life. I would even hope that some professor who did not know Christ would read that and eventually would have to call on the name of Jesus in times of help.

Out of all the years I wrote that on my test, it wasn't until my fourth year that one teacher underlined it and put "Yes!" next to it. I thought it was great just to know that my teacher knew Christ and was excited like I was. After that, we later opened up and spoke about what he wrote. It turn out he was a faith-filled believer. For some reason, I felt at ease asking questions, going to his office hours, and talking to him ever since I discovered he was a believer. It is great when you discover you have a teacher who is a Christian. I encourage you to engage your teachers to see where their faith is, because witnessing can go even far beyond your classmates.

Not only will your witness be great but your favor with the teacher will be great as well. God has given me so much favor with teachers over the years that it is ridiculous! I have had teachers that everyone said were hard to talk to, teachers that purposely failed students, and teachers that liked no one. Yet those were the teachers with whom God had given me the most favor with.

When you put God first you can obtain favor from professors in time of need. During my sophomore year I had a nice teacher, but the curriculum I had was challenging. He had a hearing problem that he mentioned to the class on the first day. That day and throughout the course the Lord had led me to pray for his ability to hear. Final exam time came, and I was not doing so well. I took the final and got a D! I had failed the course. The semester was over, but for some reason I was led to e-mail him and ask if there was anything that I could do to pass his course because I did not want to take it again. The professor said he normally did not do this, but he mailed me the final and allowed me to retake it over the summer. I turned it back into him weeks later, and he gave me a passing grade! No one had ever heard of this kind of favor because God had a specially assigned favor just for me! Start praying for your teachers and lifting up God's name. He will help you out when you are in need.

He Will Do It for You

Another thing to understand is that God is *Jehovah-jireh*, our provider. God has a provision for us corporately and individually. I had a friend give a praise report about getting an A in a physics course once. She had struggled all semester long with having just a B, and finally God prevailed at finals time. She praised God that night at the Bible study for his goodness. At the same time, I was in the same class, and I was in danger of failing the course. I had been borderline D all semester. I took the last test and I got an A on the test and a C in the class. I will never forget. Now I was praising God with her as well. Both of us received different letter grades, but it did not matter because God still provided. In addition, what makes you jump for joy may be very different than the next person. Remember to praise God for all the grades, both good and bad.

If you are experiencing academic success in college, still aim to continue to strengthen it. You may want to seek academic advice on utilizing your study time so that when you do study, you retain the most out of it. A great book that helped my academic performance was *Guaranteed 4.0* by Donna O. Johnson, a powerful woman of God. This book speaks to the study and habits of any college student and will help you develop a good practical schedule to stay "on plan" for success.

Class Notes:

1. Pray and ask God what he would have you to study.

2. Learn how to fail!

3. Remember: your GPA is important, but it does not determine who you are as child of God.

4. Apply a practical schedule to your study habits. Read *Guaranteed 4.0*

1. Do you sometimes feel like other classmates are smarter than you? Why?

_____

_____

2. Do you pray before you study and ask God to open your understanding?

_____

_____

3. What is your hardest class? Have you started praying for favor with that teacher? Start today!

_____

_____

Prayer for academic life:

Lord, I am truly grateful to have the opportunity to learn more here in college. I am blessed that you put me in a position to succeed. Help me not to get discouraged by bad test grades or missed assignments. Help me to study effectively using the right tools so that I can do well on exams. I know that your Holy Spirit brings all things to remembrance. Help me to realize that and seek knowledge. Thank you for favor with teachers and friends in study groups. I praise you in advance for high test score grades and class grades. In Jesus's name. Amen.

MY ROOMMATE HAS GOT TO BE THE DEVIL

Choosing to be a living example in your faith will help overcome the challenges of living with a roommate. You are bound to have differences with your roommate in college. Sharing your room with someone who may be of a different race, religion, background, or someone who just snores, talks in their sleep, or likes to collect beer cans under the bed for some ungodly reason will be a challenge. You are hoping to live a Christian life and now you have been thrown into a situation where you are living with someone who is an unbeliever. A conflict doesn't just arise with non-believers, but those of the same faith as well. Living with a college roommate reminds me of MTV's *The Real World*. "Watch what happens when people stop being nice and start being real!" Being real with someone should not be implied as being mean. You can be a living example to your roommate by deciding to pray when most would argue. Exercising gentleness and not judging when serious issues arise will help you represent Christ to your roommate.

Dealing with Differences

Having control over your actions and reactions is key when dealing with differences. Campus housing normally assigns everyone roommates. Random selection no doubt. Even though it may be random to you, God selected them way before campus housing. My first roommate and I were completely different. We were to share a '9x13' room. That means we would be close—literally!

As I arrived before my roommate, I took my alone time with God to meditate. As I prayed God led me to anoint the doorpost of the room and the windows, both of the beds, and the desk. After finishing I felt at peace, and that came from knowing I had taken the spiritual authority that God wanted me to have. "I have given you authority to trample on snakes and scorpions and to overcome all the power of the enemy; nothing will harm you" (Luke 10:13, NIV). I knew that in order to have peace, God's presence had to be welcomed in my dorm room.

On move-in day, my roommate showed up. He was there with the rest of his family: mother, father, and girlfriend. Within the first five minutes I knew this would be a challenge. He had this screensaver on his computer that would yell out curse words every time he clicked the mouse. He even cursed back at his mother when she asked him to shut it off and introduce himself to me. It was awkward; one of the nightmare situations you dread when finding out who your roommate is. I asked myself, *What kind of guy disrespects his mom like that?* He didn't seem interested to know anything about me, so I came in, straightened up a little bit, and then left. As I was walking to football practice, I prayed. I asked God to remove him, if it was in his will, from my room as my roommate

That night I slept in the room. My roommate actually had his girlfriend spend the night over (I know, on the first night!). It was so uncomfortable. The next night, he came in. He started to fold his clothes and put them in a suitcase. He turned and said that he was moving out and joining a frat house. I was amazed! Not at him leaving but at how quickly God had heard my prayers. Thank you, Jesus! I tried to play it cool, but when God hears you and answers you, you just can't help but smile and laugh to yourself all at the same time.

That entire freshman year I continued to have the spiritual authority over my room. I had another two roommates after him. They didn't last long either. One was of a different religion who knew I actually knew something about the Bible. I guess he had fear of being converted, so he left. The other had a serious drinking problem. One day he walked in on me while I was praying, so I began to pray for him and his drinking habit. The very next week, he left too.

For the majority of the year I had a room to myself. It was great! All that alone time with God and just unlimited prayer time was wonderful. I didn't have it this way because I was rude, judgmental, or had a "holier-than-thou" attitude. I was just simply being God's child, and he took care of me.

What I realized then was that the purpose for having a roommate is not necessarily for you to find a friend. Don't get me wrong, having a roommate can be great. It would present itself as an opportunity for twenty-four-seven evangelism to someone who may not know Jesus. Sure, it would be easy to tell your roommate you need Jesus and not have to live with them, but here is someone who sees all of your habits and probably watches you very critically. Initially when I entered college, it was never my intention to run all three of my roommates off my first year. I just wanted to be able to live my life as a young believer, comfortably in my room. Paul told Timothy some words of wisdom that we can use. He said, "Keep a close watch on how you live and on your teaching. Stay true to what is right for the sake of your own salvation and the salvation of those who hear you" (1 Timothy 4:16, NLT).

So we now know what may be the purpose when it comes to a mixed environment with believer and non-believer roommates. Yet what is the purpose when there are two believers as roommates? The misconception that many believers assume is that if two Christians live together, things will automatically go great. This is not always true. Two different people still means two different living habits and two sets of issues.

Addressing Issues the Right Way

My sophomore year I got an apartment off campus with an old teammate and fellow minister. I figured that after my freshman year experience with roommates being unbelievers, nothing would be more comfortable than having a saved roommate. It was just the opposite. For the first few months, we rarely spoke. Our schedules barely had us crossing paths. When we did speak it was in a harsh tone about bad cleaning habits, unexpected visitors, or paying the bills on time. For the whole first year, everything was a conflict. Eventually we faced each other one day and just had it out. We said what we didn't like and what we expected out of a roommate. We then prayed and asked God to help our living situation. From that point on, we began to understand our purpose as roommates. It actually turned into a very powerful ministry partnership between both of us. We went from not speaking to one another, to daily praying with each other. We also attracted those who lived within our complex to the ministry we had going on in that apartment. The expectation that I had of my roommate came later, but it was a blessing when it did happen.

Another instance occurred during my graduating senior year. One of my roommates would have his girlfriend over every night. They would stay in the basement most of the time, but every now and again she would use our kitchen, refrigerator, laundry, and even our shower! She was practically living there. It became an inconvenience, and I was led to say something. I prayed over it and asked God to give me what to say. So one day I sat down and had a talk with my roommate, who was also a believer, and told him that I wasn't trying to police his life, but that he couldn't continue to have his girlfriend sleep there every night. As I spoke to him I felt I came in love and gentleness, not in judgment. Even though I thought I addressed things the right way he was still in shock. He still decided to move out. However, I felt that I had addressed the issue properly. "If another believer sins against you, go privately and point out the offense" (Matthew 18:15, NLT). Correcting another believer should be done in private. I didn't broadcast to the other roommates what our issue was. I addressed it directly with him. Doing the right thing always pays off, even if you don't get the right response initially.

Don't always assume that things just work out with roommates. We are human beings with differences and similarities. It takes Christ to bring things together. When you choose to be a living example and to address living issues with your roommate in a peaceful manner, God will bless your living environment. "Be patient, bearing with one another in love. Make every effort to keep the unity of the Spirit through the bond of peace" (Ephesians 4:2-3, NIV).

Class Notes:

Steps to take if your roommate is a non-believer:

1. Pray and begin to take spiritual authority over the room

2. Next, observe their habits. Can you live with some of them? I knew immediately that if my roommate disrespected his parents, he would definitely disrespect me and my space. So it was a no-go!

3. Ask God to remove them. Then, trust him, because he will!

1. Have you made an effort to adapt to your roommate and living conditions, or would you say that you have compromised yourself in any way?

_____

_____

2. Have you taken a chance on taking spiritual authority over your room?

_____

_____

3. Do you feel as though you can no longer live with your roommate and that you need to ask God to remove them from your living space?

_____

_____

Steps to take if you are not getting along with a Christian roommate:

1. Understand that even though both of you love Jesus, it has nothing to do with your living habits. My roommate used to say, "I know you're saved and everything, but I need you to do the dishes."

2. Next, pray that God gives purpose to your living together. When you understand your purpose is far beyond just getting affordable rent, you are more apt to put up with more.

3. Next, join your roommate in prayer for any attacks of the enemy that may come between you and that attempt to interfere in God's purpose.

Prayer for roommate:

Lord God, I recognize that in all you do there is a purpose. Show me the purpose for my roommate. Why are they here at this time in my life? What should I be saying? How should I carry myself? Help me to resist any habits or traits that they may bring that are unlike you. Help me to live a real life of faith before him/her in order they may see the light that you have placed within me. In Jesus's name. Amen.

JESUS KNOWS HOW TO PARTY!

I kept repeating to myself as I prayed, "To whom much is given, much is required" (Luke 12:48, KJV). However, it seemed like sometimes it just wasn't fair. I wanted to dance, hang out with friends, but there were some parties and places God would not allow me to go. At the time, I just thought God was trying to be unfair, but eventually he showed me that he was protecting my character and preserving my integrity. "Do not be misled: Bad company corrupts good character" (1 Corinthians 15:33, NIV). Establishing limits and finding accountable friends will allow you to party without compromise. Attending parties for a reason will also help you keep your character. Character is important to guard, yet for those who still decide to party, it is equally important not to judge others who do. Finding a balance between fun and integrity is one that requires wise choices.

Accountability Keeps You Out of Trouble

Making wise choices takes godly accountable friends. Friends will uphold and remind each other that you represent Christ even at the party. When we see Jesus attending the wedding celebration, we see that he took his disciples with him (John 2:2, NIV). He took those who were close to him. It is best for you to take your "inner circle" of friends to hold you accountable for your actions. When we are alone and feel like no one is watching us, we will do all types of things. Accountability should be in the air when we attend events with friends. These are the same faithful friends with whom we have shared prayer and Bible study lessons together, so it would be inappropriate for us to go somewhere and become *Christians gone wild*. Do you know the phrase "friends don't let friends drive drunk,"? Well, "friends don't let friends party without accountability."

Jesus went to the party with a purpose. Jesus wanted to celebrate the wedding. He did not come to get drunk. He did not go to the party to get high. Many of the parties in college are more than just a good time. I would have gladly gone to many of those parities if it didn't mean spiked punch or lots of smoking. It was an offensive environment that I didn't like. The environment at the wedding feast did not offend Jesus. The environment should not offend you as well. If it does, leave!

Most of the time, we have a hard time not going to special events because we know that everybody is going to be there and we feel left out by not going. As a freshman

I thought that if I did not go, the upperclassmen would not think I was cool, especially when a senior invited me out. So, I would go. I did not go because there was a purpose, but because of the social pressure that surrounded it. Most freshmen who enter college are still trying to find their place. They do not know if they want to pledge or rush or know with whom they should hang out with. Most of the time I went in hopes that maybe I would see a cute girl. Yet I should have refused and just been my own person. Don't be afraid to be different. Remember, God made us peculiar, which means we are special to him, chosen for something greater. (1 Peter 2:9, KJV).

Keep Your Character

Not being mindful of your character at parties can ruin your witness. Jesus did not let parties mess up his witness. After Jesus performed the miracle of turning water into wine at the party, it actually confirmed God's glory. The party did not compromise his witness; it promoted it (John 2:9-10, KJV). Many times I have been hesitant to go to certain events, not because I did not want to, but because of my witness. Being not only a Christian but also a young minister on my campus, I had to guard my witness. By attending the events, I would have put myself in bad company, causing my character to be corrupted. This may have ultimately hindered my witness to someone at a crucial point in his or her life. If I have to sacrifice a party in order for someone to receive salvation, then so be it. "Watch your life and doctrine closely.

Persevere in them, because if you do, you will save both yourself and your hearers" (1 Timothy 4:16, MSG).

I also know many Christians who see nothing wrong with partying. They do it quite frequently and have not compromised their faith or their beliefs. Yet many have told me that they have eased back on prayer time and study time with God. Another factor to consider is when to stop partying and start praying? How much time do I spend partying, and how much time do I spend with God? Many times, sin or "backsliding" is not as evident as we see it. If last semester you would spend an hour praying and talking to God, but this semester you are only giving him five to ten minutes, then something in your relationship with God has changed, and it may not be a change for the best. Your subtraction of time commitment has happened because something else has come into your life that has pulled you away from God.

So what is the solution? We want to hang out, but we do not want to compromise. If there is a group of Christian students on your campus that feel like this, then start your own party. I have attended many Christian parties that have been a great time and fellowship. We would play contemporary gospel/Christian rock, play board games, and watch the latest gospel play on DVD, which was a great time for us. Just because we are in the world does not mean we have to be of this world. Find others who are willing to step out and do something different. However, don't judge those who may still be a work in progress because we all are.

Don't Judge, Just Pray

My first semester, my friend Veronica seemed to not only be at every Bible study, but every party as well. At one of the parties that I attended, I overheard her and some girls talking about going to get something to drink. These girls were older, and I felt they were a bad influence on her. I wanted to pull her to the side that night and tell her not to go, but I did not. A few weeks later in Bible study, I remember crying during prayer because I knew she was such a powerful woman of God, and I also knew God had a strong anointing over her life. That next semester was different. Veronica had quit the drinking habit and was even more on fire for the Lord. It was not until three years later I brought up that night and told her how I felt. She told me, "You know, if you had said something that night, I probably wouldn't have received it, and I would have thought you were judging me." She then said, "I had to come to God on my own time." This is so true. Do not force anyone to stop doing what he or she is doing. Let the Holy Spirit do his work in that person's life. As for those Christians who are not currently partying right now but instead are talking about those Christians who do, know that you haven't always been saved and God "despises a proud look" (Proverbs 6:17, KJV). For those friends you feel that should not be going to the party, begin to pray for them, and do not confront them unless the Lord leads you.

Class Notes:

Jesus Knows how to party rules:

1. Make sure you go to the party with your "inner circle" of accountable friends.

2. Go to the party for a purpose.

3. Make sure the party does not compromise your character.

4. Make sure that partying is not interrupting your relationship with God.

5. Don't judge fellow Christians who may still be partying.

6. Pray for them and let the Holy Spirit do his work.

1. Who do you think will keep you accountable in a compromising situation? And why?

_____

_____

2. Do you have a different character at parties than in your normal, everyday life? If so, evaluate that different characteristic compared to a godly character.

_____

_____

3. Is your relationship with God or anything else affected by your partying habits?

_____

_____

Prayer for "Jesus Knows How to Party":

Lord, I know you made me in your image, and in all I do I should seek to reflect you. Help me to be the salt of the earth and the light of the world that you called me to be. I see others who are partying and having a good time, but they are not glorifying your name. At times I admit I feel like I am missing out, but I know that life will fade. Surround me, God, with great friends who share my faith so that we can still enjoy this life together and not feel like we have to compromise in order to have fun. In Jesus's name. Amen.

WAKE UP! IT'S TIME TO GO TO CHURCH!

I must have called at least three times. I decided to give it one more try.

"Hello?" Samantha whispered. I could tell she was still asleep.

"Hey, Samantha!" I said. "Are you still going to church?"

I had invited Samantha the last couple of weeks. She really enjoyed the first time we went, but that had been almost three months ago.

"I...I don't think so. I gotta do some studying today and some other things." This sounded like many of the other excuses I had heard before.

"Okay," I said in disappointment. "Talk to you later."

I often got frustrated throughout my college years as I continued to try to invite more of my friends to go to church. It seemed like I had heard every excuse. From, "I don't have any church clothes" to "I have a lot of tests this week." Parties, studying, and clothes are not excuses to get between us and worshiping the God who loves us.

Choosing to be faithful to a ministry while in college is necessary to your spiritual growth. Lifeway Researchers found that 70 percent of teens who attended a church regularly (twice a month or more) in high school stopped attending church regularly for at least one year between ages of eighteen to twenty-two. There are many reasons college students stop going, from life changes to location. However, we are still called to be in the assembly of the saints while in college. "And let us not neglect our meeting together" (Hebrew 10:25, NLT). There is no substitute for a place of worship with other believers. Finding that right place and staying faithful may be a challenge, but if you make the right choice you please God in doing so.

So, Why Don't We Go to Church?

Lifeway Researchers found that as individuals transition from adolescence to adulthood, they become more committed to religion, and their religious beliefs become more genuine; in contrast, their attendance at religious services actually decreases. Over 52 percent of students stop going to church because of a change in religious, ethical, or political beliefs. Whereas religious practices may have been prescribed by family while living at home, once away at college, individuals may have more opportunities to examine different religions and beliefs. In addition, individuals may feel that church is too judgmental or think that church members are unfriendly. Whatever the reason, there is a sense of disconnect with the church in the transition years of college.

It's very different when your parents are knocking on your door to wake you up for Sunday school. At the beginning, independence means, "I don't have to go to church." One time I was at a seminar and the minister asked how many people went to church before college. The whole room seemed to raise their hands. Then he asked, "How many people go to church now?" A little over a quarter of the people in the room raised their hands. The minister went on to expound that many students who go to college stop going to church not because they don't love Jesus, but because it was forced upon them when they were back at home. Now since they are away from home, they have rebelled against home, and church is a part of that rebellion. Lifeway researchers show that 27 percent of students want a break from church. They see that church, Jesus, and God are something that can be reserved for later. However, college students should know that you can't just take a break from being a Christian for a few years.

Don't Fall into Artificial Worship

Some of my friends have even told me, "I don't need to attend church because I have church right there in my living room." A large amount of my friends conveniently attend online worship ceremonies or find them in front of the television screen. Now don't get me wrong; I believe that God's divine Word can come through the radio waves or television and convict the heart as if you were in any pew. "For the word of God is living and active. Sharper than any double-edged sword, it penetrates even to dividing soul and spirit, joints and marrow; it judges the thoughts and attitudes of the heart" (Hebrews 4:12, NIV). However, as I mentioned earlier, there is accountability that comes with fellowshipping with other believers. Even when the early church was coming together in the book of Acts, they understood the importance of being in fellowship.

> And all the believers lived in a wonderful harmony, holding everything in common. They sold whatever they owned and pooled their resources so that each person's need was met. They followed a daily discipline of worship in the Temple followed by meals at home, every meal a celebration, exuberant and joyful, as they praised God. People in general liked what they saw. Every day their number grew as God added those who were saved.
>
> Acts 2:44-47 (MSG)

Here we see the close fellowship of the believers. This would certainly have not occurred if all of the members of the church signed on, but when they were tired signed off. You have to be careful when worship becomes too convenient, because you may not be experiencing true worship. After the split of Israel there was the northern and the southern kingdom. Rehoboam, Solomon's son, lived in the northern kingdom where Jerusalem is located.

Yet Jeroboam abides in Dan and Bethel in the southern kingdom. Because Jeroboam was fearful that he would lose his position as king, he decided to create a false sense of worship for the people. "So the king came up with a plan: he made two golden calves. Then he announced, "It's too much trouble for you to go to Jerusalem to worship. Look at these—the gods who brought you out of Egypt! He put one calf in Bethel; the other he placed in Dan" (1 Kings 12:28, MSG). So the people began to worship the golden calves because it was closer and less of a journey. Yet real worship was in Jerusalem. Let's not simply roll over and give God convenient worship, but let's give him true worship. "Yet a time is coming and has now come when the true worshipers will worship the Father in spirit and truth, for they are the kind of worshipers the Father seeks" (John 4:23, NIV).

Why Do We Need to Go to Church?

"Faith comes by hearing and hearing the Word of God" (Romans 10:17, KJV). In order to receive the faith that pleases God, you must be in an area where you can hear from God. "And how shall they hear without a preacher?" (Romans 10:14 KJV). There is not some type of magic in the building that cancels all our problems, but it is because we are actually the church, the body of believers. In my opinion if other college students would see the benefit of getting underneath God's Word, fellowshipping with other believers, and being held accountable by a pastor, then they would not be so easily defeated.

I had a guy once tell me, "I want to go to church, but I just can't wake up on time!" If staying up late and partying affects your time with God on Sundays, then don't go to the party. Make the sacrifice: do not go or leave early. It is upon you to do it. "Work out your own salvation with fear and trembling" (Philippians 2:12, KJV). Quickly I dispelled the time issue with church because I attended a church that started at noon. Wow! Even this did not help because many students would still find themselves not wanting to go. In my opinion, those who would show up would only do it for what God could do for them. "Though you honor me with your lip service, your hearts are far from me" (Matthew 15:8, NIV). Simply put, many ask God for good grades. Yet, your relationship with God was never intended to simply give you good grades. "Seek you first the kingdom of heaven, and all these things shall be added unto thee" (Matthew 6:33, KJV). Your relationship was intended to give you all things. Nevertheless, you have to wholeheartedly serve him without any other motives.

Again, it is so vital to fellowship with other faith-filled believers. By hearing their testimonies, I become encouraged as well. This is also God's way to show you that you are not in this alone and that whatever you are going through, someone has gone through it before you. There was no better memory in my college life than to hear the praise reports we would do before Monday night Bible study. It was better than any reality series because I was actually in touch with the characters around me. It was amazing to hear what God was doing among his people. Yet I would have never heard these beautiful testimonies unless I had been around other saved friends. Don't let minor excuses keep you from major blessings. Being in college places you in a role of independence. Now it is upon you to know and seek God for yourself. Your relationship with him was established at home, but it was meant to flourish while in college. By attending church while in college, you affirm your independent relationship with God. Your mother, father, and no else who is around you can force you to go to church. Continue in the faith and bring other classmates that need to be in church and have a relationship with Christ as well.

Be a Light to Someone Else

Witnessing is a process that requires patience and a consistent living of your faith. Some of you may be frustrated about a close friend or classmate that you have been trying to get to attend church the entire semester or year. Each week I continued to call those friends I wanted to attend church, and I would offer to pick them up and even promise food after the service. What I was doing was good, but it was too much of my own effort. When it came down to it, my friends never went all the times I kept asking and asking. One Sunday I just showed up, and to my surprise, they were there. I didn't call, and I didn't have to force them. What I did do was plant a seed. As college student it is our responsibility to be seed planters in the lives of those friends around us. "I have planted, Apollos watered; but God gave the increase" (1 Corinthians 3:6, KJV).

A good example of a seed growing was when one time I was shooting pool with my friend Adam, and he said something that opened my eyes. I had noticed that he had been coming to Bible study and church. He was a graduate student I asked him, "What made you start coming to church?"

He said, "There comes a time in an every man's life when he has to get close to God." What we must realize is that we should just let life happen when it comes to people. No one will ever fall in love with God if you force them. Think about it. Did you? However, something will occur in their lives like a death in the family, a bad break-up, or it maybe even a bad semester or test grade. Whatever it is, God knows how to bring them back to him. "I have drawn you with loving-kindness" (Jeremiah 31:3, NIV) Continue to pray for them and trust God. When he's ready for them to come, he will draw them near. Don't force church on people. When you do, it resurfaces issues that they may have had back at home with being forced to go to church. Just let life happen. Sooner or later they will see the need in finding a church home and church family.

Finding and Committing
to the Right Church

You have made up in your heart and mind you want to go to church, but where? You have to begin to socialize with other believers. *How do I find other believers?* Going to the campus Bible study. Asking around where others attend church is a good way to locate a potential church home. I suggest you attend a few at the beginning, getting a good sense for the culture and spiritual atmosphere of the church. Then, just ask God. *God, where would you have me to worship? God, where can I grow as young Christian for the next years of my life?* Then, let God talk to you. He will confirm your interest in a church with his voice and others around you as well.

After you have found that church home, the goal is commitment. Church is just like the classroom. Yes, you show up to gain and receive spiritual knowledge, but it is not where you show up just to be on the roll and in attendance. Commitment to a church means to invest time in the ministry that God would have for you at that church. God has given each and every one of us a spiritual gift. One of the first things that my college pastor said to me was, "I am glad to have you here at this church. Know that your gift here will make room for you." Over the years I have come to understand that by committing to my college church and devoting my gift to the service of the Lord, I was enriched even more. Your college church becomes a training ground for what God has for you even after you leave college. Committing time to your church within your college schedule will pay off. At our church, we would have the opportunity to minister to the poor, to witness in the prison ministry, to take church road trips to concerts, and to enjoy many holiday dinners together. Truly, I remember these times of my college life more than any test, grade, or quizzes.

When you become committed to a church, giving is a part of that commitment a well. By understanding the principles of tithing, God can bless us even as "broke college students." When I was a sophomore in high school, I began to tithe. At first I did it because I knew my pastor and church leaders said it was right. Yet later I began to read God's Word and really gain a personal understanding. "Bring me the very best of the first harvest to the house of the Lord your God" (Exodus 23:19, NLT). By giving God my increase at a young age, he continued to bless me. Once I got into college, I continued my worship through giving to God. I would give my tithes to my college church, and knowing that we were trying to grow the ministry, I would devote as much as I could in my offering. I'll never forget the pastor's wife of my local church came up to me after service. She asked me to get a few things out of her car. When I got to the car there were bags and bags of groceries—more than a week worth. She told me to put the bags in my car. Wow! What a blessing! This was at a time when my money was low and I couldn't afford food. God knew just how to bless me and who to send. All this was a result of being committed to tithing, even as a college student. Understand that God is "no respecter of persons." Simply put, even college students must tithe. Being Christian college students, it is our duty to serve our God who has blessed us. Deuteronomy 15:10 (NIV) says, "Give generously to him and do so without a grudging heart; then because of this the Lord your God will bless you in all your work and in everything you put your hand to.

Class Notes:

"Wake Up! It's Time to Go to Church!"

1. Pray and ask God to take away any spirit of rebellion. (You may also ask closer "inner circle" friends to pray as well.)

2. Identify a local church or local Bible study where you can grow spiritually from the Word, from the worship, and the fellowship.

3. Don't make excuses when it comes to being in the assembly of other believers.

4. Be patient with friends who you invite, and know that they will come in God's timing.

5. Become seed planters in college for those who don't know Christ.

6. Commit to your college church and ministry.

7. Commit to tithing and receive the blessing from God.

1. Why haven't you been attending church?

_____

_____

2. If you are not at the moment attending a local church while at school, have you taken the necessary steps, like praying about it and asking known Christian friends of possible churches that you can attend?

_____

_____

3. Do you think your friends become offended when you ask them to come to church? And do you feel disappointed when a friend doesn't show up?

_____

_____

Prayer for church attendance:

Lord, we know that you desire for us to fellowship with others in the body of Christ. We also know that you have created us to worship you and give you glory. Help us to see the true meaning of being a worshiper while still in college. Help us not to fall into a lazy mindset or start to make excuses. But let your commitment to your church carry us through our college years and beyond. In Jesus's name. Amen.

ARE YOU MY
REAL FRIEND?

Selecting the right friends builds the necessary support when faced with rough times. Right now on Facebook, I think I have 1,293 friends. That's not a lot compared to some other people I know. But how many could I call and pray with if I needed prayer? Or if I was trying to go deeper in God, could I actually fast with them? Sure you can tag me, add me, or poke me, but the truth is real friends are hard to find. In order to find real friends, you have to first define what real friendship is. Determine the qualities of real friendship can on only be found by looking to God's Word. Authentic friends refuse to stay away in times of trouble. They share in your pain. They don't point blame you when you are down. After looking to God's Word to define your relationships, you will reevaluate who you call "friends."

Define Real Friendship

So how many friends do you really need? Twenty, ten, five, or one? The Word says that a friend should be closer than a brother. Jesus also lets us know that "Greater love has no man than to lay down his life for his friends" (John 15:13, NIV). One essential quality of friendship requires sacrifice. I can testify that my close friends sacrificed their time, money, and effort in order to make sure that I was okay.

Friends are open with each other about feelings and wishes. In John 15:9, Jesus wasn't slow about showing his love for his friends. Not only did he show his love, but in Matthew 17:7 he showed his anger when his disciples did not have the faith to heal someone. Real friendship is a open door. You don't have to keep secrets and you don't fear being judged by that person. Being able to share without feeling judged will encourage you with the love of God.

A true friend encourages you to develop and to use your talents for God. Jesus said, "You didn't choose me. I chose you. I appointed you to go and produce lasting fruit, so that the Father will give you whatever you ask for, using my name" (John 15:16, NLT). Jesus wanted his followers to use their talents to make a lasting difference. Your friends should push you to use your gifts for the kingdom. A real friend will not let you be lazy and sit down when the kingdom can benefit from your gift. Friends also push each others to do more. If a person does not exhibit these characteristics, then you should watch who you call your friend.

I think one of the loosest words we use as college students is *friends*. Everyone is "friend" this or "friend" that. Understand that it took Jesus three and half years before he called the disciples "friends." "I'm no longer calling you servants because servants don't understand what their master is thinking and planning. No, I've named you friends because I've let you in on everything I've heard from the Father" (John 15:15, MSG). Jesus could no longer call the disciples servants because they had gone through some experience with him. These experiences earned them the title of friend.

Find a Real Friendship

Life experience will develop friendships. Most people always ask, "How do you find great friends?" And it really has no set formula. Some will meet on the same floor in the dorms, in the same class, or in the choir together. It may even be a non-believer who introduces you to some of your best Christian friends. What you should understand is that you will never find those "inner circle" friends if you do not interact with others. Please don't be like I was for my first three weeks of college. I somehow thought that if I was to maintain my Christianity on campus, it would require me to be a spiritual hermit. I spent the first three weeks going to football practice, to class, then to my dorm room. I didn't really want to interact with many people until one night at a campus picnic. I started talking to a couple of other guys on campus.

These guys were older than me. To this day I can't even remember how the conversation started, but four hours later, I felt like we were all best friends. It turned out that every guy in the circle, all five of us, just so happened to be ministers. I didn't wake up that day saying, "I am going to go find other ministers on campus are and strike up a biblical conversation." I was primarily going to the picnic to get something to eat. Those same five guys are still my close friends to this day, and that was over eight years ago.

If I had to give spiritual advice for finding friends, it would be life experience. Simply experience life and you will see who shows up to be there for you. Try not to expect much out of those who are not friends, but when you do have friends come into your circle, hold them accountable as you should in Christ. "His spirit was knit with Jonathan" (1 Samuel 18:1, KJV). David and Jonathan had such a close friendship that even when Saul was trying to kill David because of his jealousy, Jonathan still defended him and took up for him. Even in the face of danger and life-threatening issues, real friends will stand out and shine through tough times.

Real Friendship Will Be Tested

A true friendship will be tested. In Job 6:14-21 (NIV), we see that Job's three friends show up in Job's time of need. Here Job had been an good man and had nothing wrong in his life (Job 1:1, NLT). When his three friends showed up, Job had lost his children and home. His wife had cursed God. In short, his whole life was in a mess. Job was in an incredibly tough time. Job's friend's did three things well in his time of crisis that are also important to notice in your real friendships.

The first thing they did well was coming to him when he needed them. They did not stay away, as some people do, saying things to themselves like, "I won't know what to say" or "what if I say the wrong thing?" If you are going through a bad day—maybe you received a bad test grade or broke up with your college sweetheart—you need your friends there.

The second thing they did well was being silent yet present. When Job's friends showed up they didn't try to offer words. They just simply were there. Maybe you are in school and you have a friend who lost a parent, grand-parent, or close family member. Sometimes there are no words to express what a grieving person needs. Yet, your presence shows you care.

The third thing they did well was weep with him. "Rejoice with them that do rejoice, and weep with them that weep" (Roman 12:15, KJV). Job's friend's feelings were in sync with his. Good friends don't laugh when you are crying. When you hurt, they are hurt. If you are a struggling in a class, a good friend won't laugh at your difficulties; they'll help you study and work through the problems to get you better.

Class Notes:

"Are You My Real Friend?":

1. Define a real friendship and the attributes that they should possess.

2. Find a real friendship through life experiences.

3. Understand that friends openly express the depth of their feelings.

4. Understand that friends understand your issues, so they say very little at times.

1. Have you ever made it a point to bring God up during a conversation to see if the person you were speaking to was also a Christian?

_____

_____

2. Does your circle of Christian friends pray for each other or hold each other accountable?

_____

_____

3. Do your friends put you before them, and do you put your friend's needs before your own?

_____

_____

Prayer for real friends:

Lord, help us to have a discerning spirit for the friends that we meet on campus. Help us to know who is our close friend and who may be our enemies. There will be many out there that will wish to deceive us, but please reveal their intentions to us. For the close friends we do have, help us to build one another up in the faith. In Jesus's name. Amen.

CAMPUS LOVE LIFE

Relationships while in college can interfere with your studies if you don't use precaution and set appropriate guidelines. Dating can be a distraction and destructive if you don't have marriage in mind. Casual dating will oftentimes lead to premature intimacy. Adding intimacy without godly commitment will lead to unnecessary stress. This stress will distract you from your purpose for education. However, if you make the choice to date with marriage in mind and follow godly guidelines, you can have a healthy relationship in college.

Many Christians only want to know three questions about dating: "Who can I date?" "How far can I go?" "Who can I marry?"

Who Can I Date?

So "Who can you date?" is easy. Only date someone who shares your faith and could be a potential future mate. Dating is about marriage, not to find a cuddle buddy. We choose who we date by how good they look, when looks will fade. We base lifetime decisions on the fact that we like the same shows on MTV or the same song at the time. Only those things may change. You have to choose someone who shares your love for Christ and loves God even more than they love you.

Hanging out in groups helps you discover hidden characteristics about a person you may not find in traditional dating. Many times we jump into a dating relationship prematurely because we think that is the only way to get to know someone. Being one on one with someone at the beginning of your relationship actually hinders getting to know them because they tend to send their representative. Yes, everyone has an ambassador. One of my campus jobs was to be a student ambassador. I was paid to say nice things about the school. Even if I didn't like something about the school, as an ambassador I kept my mouth shut because I didn't want folks to be deterred from coming to school there—nor did I want to lose my job. When you date one on one at the beginning, you are meeting their ambassador. Sure it seems like sparks are flying and you two are a match made in heaven. But let's see how this person really acts when around his frat brothers or her sorority sisters. Let's see if he is obnoxious or if she is rude to others. As time goes by, God will reveal to you how they really are.

God made us to want companionship and to not want to be alone, yet in the right context of marriage. From my experience, when we do start dating seriously someone in college, it becomes much like a "play" marriage. It starts casually by making dinner together a few nights a week. Then we start doing laundry over at each other's place, until we finally start sleeping over at each other's apartments. I have even seen college couples who have signed leases together and shared cell phone plans. These are things that God reserved for marriage. Being one is not something you play around with. I remember knowing a senior couple on campus who shared an apartment and had every class together. They spent four years doing that! Oddly enough three months before graduation, they broke up. Think about how devastating that was. Imagine how it might be to have spent all of those years with someone and then end it. You would feel, in a sense, like a part of your life had been wasted. Think about all of the healthy friendships and relationships that could have been forming had they not been so attached to one another.

Dating isolates you from other friendships. Oftentimes we are so wrapped up into a person that we forget about our other close friends. We stop hanging out with the fellas (or ladies) because we are joined at the hip with someone. Don't let a brief fling or even long-term dating relationship hinder other great friendships. Remember, your friendships are going to be there with you through ups and downs. What do you say about your friendships when you push them to the side for a relationship that may not last?

How Far Can I Go?

So let me be clear and up front. You can't have sexual intercourse. You can't do anything resembling sexual intercourse. Many of my classmates have always tried to find loopholes in God's divine plan for sex. "Does oral sex count as sex?" "Does full-body grinding with clothes on count as sex?" Let's not kid ourselves. You know the answers. Remember your body is temple of God's spirit. Why would you want to subject God's Holy Spirit to any of our nastiness?

Our flesh often tries to get us to compromise and forget about God's spirit in us. When we put ourselves into compromising situations it aids our flesh's agenda to compromise. Late-night movies on the sofa aren't the best spots to say, "No, let's not have sex." Your flesh is already in the position it wants to be—alone without any accoutability. It will bend all of God's rules just to meet its needs. That why the Word says "flee." When Joseph was in Potiphar's house and Potiphar's wife began to come on to him, he didn't stop and say "Let's pray about this." He got up and ran. Flee from fornication. You have to get up run away and not look back—even if it means leaving your clothes.

If you do choose to engage in premarital sex during college, it will only add to the burden of academics. Having to worry about if you are pregnant is nothing you want to do during finals week. Wondering if your boyfriend/girlfriend has given you an STD is additional worry that will distract your focus from school. Read 2 Samuel 11. David was out of position when he stayed behind out of the war. When you find yourself out of place, you will get distracted from your purpose. David then let Bathsheba take his attention. David engaged in a relationship that led to lying, adultery, and murder. David reaped later consequences for his bad choices. Don't let your college relationship lead you into the consequences of bad grades, failing classes, or even worse, dropping out of school. Your best bet is to make Jesus your focus while in college.

Who Can I Marry?

You have to marry someone who would make a good spouse. I know that sounds easy, but the hard part is developing criteria for what a good spouse is. In order to do that, you must go to the Word of God. "Christ gave Himself for the church, and the church follows Christ as her head, in the same way, the husband must give himself for his wife, and the wife must follow her husband" (Paraphrased from Ephesians 5:22-33). The hard part is how you figure all of this out between tests, pizzas, and football games.

When you are really serious about getting married to someone, you have to set the right environment to see their character. The Word says the husband should love his wife like Christ. Wow! What a responsibility. So the first thing is to look for someone who believes in sacrifice and knows how to show humility. Humility can be noticed through volunteering together at a shelter. See if your future spouse is active in ministry. Notice how they spend their time. Do they pursue a deeper relationship with Christ, or are they just content with where they are in him?

The Word calls the wife to follow the headship of the husband. One word I know we avoid is *submissive*. It just hits a nerve every time the discussion comes up. However, being submissive is merely having your strength under control. As a wife, when you submit to your husband, you are doing it out of reverence to God. Some questions you can ask yourself as a woman are: *Is the man I have in mind capable of giving himself for me, and is he someone I can follow?* If you're a man, ask yourself this one: *Will the woman I have in mind be capable of accepting my leadership, and is she someone I can give myself for?* If more college couples took the time to answer these two questions, so many relationship breakups and heartaches could be avoided. After asking yourself those questions, if the characteristics that you see in that person don't match up, then you know to stop dating them, because you will only waste your time.

Jesus Should Be Your College Sweetheart

The most fulfilling relationship you can have in college is with Jesus. I know that sounds corny to some and even like a cliché; however, a strong relationship with Christ will not bring unnecessary worries and will bring fulfillment that you can't find in anyone else. College is a great starting ground for a deeper relationship, because you are apart from everyone back home. Use this time wisely to become secure in yourself and satisfied in present circumstances.

Your status on Facebook is not a reflection on your status with God. Just because you see many of your friends pop up on your live feed with "in a relationship," and now they have multiple pictures of them and the new boyfriend/girlfriend. This doesn't mean that they are happy. This can be at times superficial or social happiness because it appeals to everyone. Everyone would like to have someone; however, you have the opportunity to have *the one*. Too bad they don't have a status that just says, "I'm content." That would have been Paul's status. Actually, I don't have a sense of needing anything personally. I've learned by now to be quite content whatever my circumstances (Philippians 4:11, MSG).

Sometimes returning to Jesus comes after being in disappointing relationships. After years of dating and making time for everyone else, time by myself seemed weird. I thought something was wrong with me to be in on a Friday night. I felt I should be road tripping somewhere or just doing anything besides being alone. Yet I began to laugh and just enjoyed the simplicity in my relationship with Christ.

It seems in other relationships you have to pretend to be someone else in order to be accepted by that person. Almost like a reality series, you are trying to prove that you are qualified to be with them, so you do things you don't normally do to win them over. However, Jesus wants you just the way you are and accepts you. He knows you're a mess. "For all have sinned and fall short of the glory of God" (Romans 3:23, KJV). Yet, he still loves you. "But God demonstrated His love for us, in while we were yet sinners" (Romans 5:8, KJV). Jesus offers us to be in a relationship with him along time ago on the cross. He sent a relationship request through his Word, "That if you confess with your mouth, 'Jesus is Lord,' and believe in your heart that God raised him from the dead, you will be saved" (Romans 10:9, KJV). This is the best relationship you can ever have. A relationship that even when you fall away he will always love you.

Even in the best relationship with God, you are bound to fall sometimes. However, God always sends those to encourage us to get back into relationship with him. John told the church of Ephesus that they had been doing a great job. They had made it through tough times and did not tolerate people who did not know God around them. "Yet I hold this against you: You have forsaken your first love. Remember the height from which you have fallen! Repent and do the things you did at first" (Revelation 2:4-5, NIV). Somewhere in their relationship with God they had slacked off and needed a refreshing point. Just like your browser needs to be refreshed in order to get all the updates, so does your relationship with God. You may have been in relationship with God for years, yet it may not be as deep as it was when you first started. It's time to hit the refresh key!

Class Notes:

1.   Date someone who is a Christian and who you can see yourself marrying.

2.   Hang out in groups first to see who they really are before getting to the one-on-one dating.

3.   Traditional dating can hinder your other relationships with friends.

4.   Make Jesus your college sweetheart and hit the refresh button in your relationship.

1. Are you currently dating someone who is not a Christian? If so, why? Can you see yourself marrying him/her?

_____

_____

2. Are you dating someone who is a Christian? Can you see yourself marrying him/her? List five characteristics about them that you think will still be there in twenty-five years.

_____

_____

_____

_____

_____

3. Do you feel like you and your boyfriend/girlfriend have gone too far physically? If so, what is your plan to change that?

_____

_____

4. Has your relationship with God grown stronger or weaker since you first got saved? If weaker, then how can you hit refresh and start anew in Jesus?

_____

_____

Prayer for campus love life:

Dear Lord, thank you for creating me with the ability to love you and to love others. Help me to have healthy relationships while in school that will make you proud. Keep me pure in all my actions. I'm yours. I will not put anyone else before you. You can have all of my heart, mind, body, and soul. In Jesus's name. Amen.

TESTS ARE NOT MY ONLY PROBLEM

I waited until my roommate left. I'm sure it was still there. Once his car pulled off, I jumped from the couch and began to rummage through the trash. At first I didn't see it on top, but I kept looking and looking. The dumpster smelled pretty bad, but I didn't care. I found it. I pulled out the cord and ran in the house. I plugged it into the modem. Once the computer loaded up I was back to my usual sites. Hours went by. I sat like a zombie in front the computer, clicking away and not being satisfied by the next website or the one before. When I was finished I stared at the blank screen. I thought about what I had just done. My body felt numb and lifeless. Frustrated at myself, I began to cry uncontrollably. I got out of the chair and fell on my knees and began to pray. I called out to God for hours because I hated that I was living like this. Though I didn't want to admit it, I was addicted to pornography.

Unconquered hidden addictions can become a hindrance to your faith and academics. Recognizing and admitting your issue is the beginning of deliverance. In order to walk in your deliverance you must stay away from what is affecting you and pray continually that God delivers your. Defeating a stronghold will not be easy; however, it is the choice you have to make to be free.

Admitting That You Have a Problem

For the longest I didn't call it an addiction. To me an addiction was more like drugs or alcohol. "It's only porn," I remember saying. I didn't sleep around. Who could it hurt? I bargained with myself. Well, Me! For one? It was hurting me and my relationship with God and I wouldn't admit it.

Your relationship with God will deteriorate when there is un-confessed sin in your life. "If we claim we have not sinned, we make him out to be a liar and his word has no place in our lives" (1 John 1:10, NIV). We tell God he has no place in our lives when we sin without repentance. Prayer time will become non-existent, because you don't want to go before a holy God with unholy issues. Avoiding fellowship with believers is another sign. There will not only be signs in your spiritual life but also in your academic life. There were times when I was late for class or would rush home in the middle of the day to look at a website. There were even times when I was running late for Bible study or church all because I had to get on the Internet just to see one website. The scariest feeling was not the times that I engaged in pornography and it hurt, but the times when I started to engaged in it and I didn't feel convicted anymore. That's when I knew I truly needed God to do something different in my life.

Admitting your problem to God is not confessing that you are weak but that is God is stronger than your problem. "God is faithful and just and will not put more on you than you can bear" (1 Corinthians 10:13, KJV). God knows all of our weaknesses already because he created us. Each one of us has different weaknesses in our flesh. Your issue may have nothing to do with pornography. Yet it has everything to do with your flesh. "The spirit is willing, but the flesh is weak" (Paraphrased from Matthew 26:41, KJV). God placed his Holy Spirit inside of us when we became his children. The Spirit in us is willing. Admit you have an issue so that God's Spirit can fight your battle.

Everyone has a different battle to fight, so it's important not to judge or look down at others. Before I got to college, I had never been a fan of drinking. I looked at people who got drunk very judgmentally. It wasn't until my senior year after turning twenty-one that I had a taste of my own medicine. While at a conference I decided to take not one, not two, but five shots of tequila. To this day, I think I just did it because everyone that night was drinking, and I wanted to be seen as the life of the party. That night I began to act rude, get angry, and danced inappropriately like I had lost my mind. And I had! I thought this would have never happened to me.

I thought I was immune to this type of sin. For years it had just been the "behind the scenes" pornography, but now it was something totally different, something public and embarrassing that I could not hide. For the next few months, I battled with this addiction. I would live two different lives. The good college church boy at school teaching Bible study, preaching, and knowing the Word but then going on my weekend trips only to get drunk. "Any man that knows the Word, but forgets it is like man who looks in the mirror then goes away only to forget who he is" (James 1:23-24, NIV). It wasn't until one day I was running through the airport to catch a flight on my way back home that God whispered in my ear and told me that I didn't have to live like this. If I continued to do this, I would disappoint him even more. I stopped in my running and began to cry in the airport. I had experienced another sin, and now I truly felt the struggle that others had dealt with as well.

It is important that you don't become like I was and silently judge others because they struggle with something else differently than you. In college I had encountered those who struggle with witchcraft, masturbation, homosexuality, fornication, and depression. One thing I love about Jesus is the variety of his ministry. He didn't just heal the sick but the possessed. He didn't just deal with the proud, but the fornicators as well. Jesus made sure that he touched every issue so that we knew that he could heal every issue.

Removing the Opportunity

Stronghold serves as distractions to the mind and mental focus on academia. "Casting down imaginations, and every high thing that exalteth itself again the knowledge of God, and bringing into captivity every thought to the obedience of Christ" (2 Corinthians 10:5, KJV). You need your mind's focus to be directed toward the books. If your mind begins to wander in class about your lust, then it is pulling you away from your purpose on campus. "Whatsoever things be good report, pure ... think on these things!" (Paraphased, Philippians 4:8, KJV).

You must remove all opportunities you have of sinning. When I was finally living on my own, I removed the cable completely. I thought I had finally cut all of my direct connections to pornography. I chose to give God the power. In order to engage in sin, you have to have an opportunity or space in time. Most of the time we place ourselves in the wrong environments or circumstances where our flesh compromises with the opportunity. For instance, I know many people who struggle with fornication, yet continue to do late-night movies with their boyfriend/girlfriend. I know others who struggle with drinking, yet they continue to go to the parties where everyone else will be getting drunk. I knew in my case that my lust was pornography. So I could no longer have the Internet in my house at all. That meant I would have to sacrifice cable and some of my favorite shows. I would have to go on campus a lot of the time to finish or do my assignments. I would make sure that when I was on the Internet that I was around others who would see me.

This became inconvenient to my schedule but a blessing to my spirit.

If you are truly serious about giving up your habit, you must take the opportunity away. Think about where the time and place of your habit occurs. Ask yourself, is there anyone around in this place? Consider telling a trusted friend exactly what you struggle with and when, and have that person hold you accountable for your actions.

"Brethren, if a man be overtaken in a fault, ye which are spiritual, restore such an one in the spirit of meekness..." (Galatians 6:1, KJV). Have an accountability partner that is truly in touch with God and can let you know when you are wrong. Sometimes your accountability partner may not be your best friend. You two may simply be acquainted through Bible study or choir, but this makes it better because you two have come together not for social interaction but spiritual growth.

I still remember the night I told one of my friends and campus minister, that I was struggling with pornography. It hurt just admitting that me, God's minister, was struggling with something so filthy. He was the first person in my life outside of God I had ever told that I was struggling with pornography. He prayed for me that night, and I remember feeling a burden lifted off me by just telling someone else. "Cast all your cares on me for he careth for you" (1 Peter 5:7, KJV). This care had never been vocalized, and now that I had admitted it, God sent someone to keep me accountable.

Coming before God with Your Problem

Another tactic that will frustrate the enemy's plans "to kill, steal, and destroy" is to take your addiction to the altar of God. In the Old Testament, that person that came before the altar had to die to their flesh before the holy presence of God. God didn't put a limit on the number of times that we can go the altar to ask him for help. It is our right as believers. "Let us then approach the throne of grace with confidence, so that we may receive mercy and find grace to help us in our time of need" (Hebrews 4:16, NIV). I just kept coming to the altar and crying and laying down before the Lord. It may have seemed silly to the natural eye, because each week I would find myself going back to the altar with the same sin. I struggled. Yet each time I went to the altar, I gained more confidence in the victory that I already had in Christ Jesus.

When we decide not to come to the altar, we avoid the issue with our own solutions, and our lives become like the woman with the issue of blood. Here she was suffering for twelve years with the same issue. She had visited doctors that only took all her money but didn't make her any better. After being broke, frustrated, and with no other way to turn, she decided there was no other option. In life you will realize that after you have tried other things, there is no substitute for Jesus. She decided to stop trying to fix it herself and reached out for Jesus's hem. She wanted just a piece of him so badly she didn't care that they had to push her way through the crowd to get to him.

Wanting to be healed has a tendency to make you forget about your classmates and friends around you. We have to make up in our mind that no matter how many weeks, semesters, or even years that we have been struggling with this issue, we are not going to let it keep us from coming to Jesus.

When the woman reached out for Jesus's hem, she literally grabbed after him so that she could go to another level. She may have been on the outer circle of the crowd for years, just watching but not pressing her way in. Now that she finally has the opportunity, she is willing to give more of herself to get him. Worship is a wonderful way to get past your issues. It requires that true worshipers must be "in spirit and in truth" (John 4:24, NIV). If you want more of God, you must be truthful with yourself. Stop inserting your own remedies, and reach out for Jesus.

Walking in Victory

Finally, walk in victory. When I think about walking, I think about a gradual moving forward. I had not believed in my heart that God could heal me. Instead of walking in victory, I walked in fear that, like a monster, one day my issues would come back to get me. "God did not give us the spirit of fear, but of love, power, and a sound mind" (Galatians 5:22, KJV). Once I made up my mind that I was free, nothing could hold me back because I now knew that "whom the son sets free is free indeed" (John 8:36, KJV).

Class Notes:

1. Read *Every Young Man's Battle* by Stephen Arterburn or *Every Young Woman's Battle* by Shannon Etheridge & Stephen Arterburn.

2. Admit to a trusted friend or campus minister what your struggle is and ask for prayer.

3. Be real with yourself and remove the temptation from around you. Even if it makes your life inconvenient.

4. Bring your issues to God and keep doing it until it goes away.

5. Walk in victory, and don't recall the defeats of your past.

1. Are you addicted to something that hinders your closeness with God? What is it? How long have you been struggling with it?

_____

_____

2. Who can you confide in and trust to tell them about your issue? What is stopping you from telling them? Set a date when you will talk with them.

_____

_____

Prayer for deliverance:

Lord, please deliver me from the stronghold that is hindering my walk with you. Whatever is getting in the way of giving you glory and truly worshiping you, remove it from my spirit. I also ask that you send practical principles in order that I grow through this and walk in righteousness. In Jesus's name. Amen.

MOVING FROM GRADES TO GREATNESS

He walked behind the podium and stood with a bold spirit. Assertive. Confident. The speaker exhorted the young college congregation into worship. He poured out God's Word with passion like Peter and wisdom like Paul. I felt a piercing as the Word of God hit home in my heart. He was a man after God's own heart; or as one who was pointing the way to Christ as John the Baptist yelled, "Prepare the way!" I was astonished that this man was only a senior in college—just a few years older than me. Somehow between school, a wife, and two kids, he seemed to handle greatness so well, and I could only aspire to do the same one day.

Since I started going to Rolla, it seemed as if he had taken me under his wing. He not only showed me the ropes around campus but also the spiritual ropes of life. There are some people that don't just impact the grade books, but they choose to impact the lives of others. I had the awesome chance to witness so many leaders go before me as a freshman. Not just people who were academically smart, but those who were in touch with God's voice in college.

Leaving a Legacy

Many college students miss the opportunity to impact the lives of others on their own campuses because they don't grasp the urgency of the season. The importance of leaving a legacy, a sign, a reminder of God on campus is evident in the book of Joshua. After Joshua had taken the role as leader after Moses's death, God performed the first miracle with Joshua crossing the Jordan River. After passing the Jordan, Joshua called for the priest to retrieve some stones for each of the tribes. He then instructed them to place the stones on the floor of the Jordan river.

> That this may be a sign among you, that when your children ask their fathers in time to come, saying, What mean ye by these stones? Then ye shall answer them, That the waters of Jordan were cut off before the ark of the covenant of the Lord; when it passed over Jordan, the waters of Jordan were cut off: and these stones shall be for a memorial unto the children of Israel forever.
>
> Joshua 4:7-9 (NIV)

The stones were left there as a reminder of what God could do for his people. As you prepare to leave your university, ask yourself, "What stones have I left behind? Does anyone know my vision and all that I really wanted to accomplish for this campus?" Be sure to carry your stone and place them so that they might be a sign. So when others ask about how you made it through certain ups and down of college, you can point to the miracle of God as the legacy you are leaving.

A campus leader must have certain characteristics. A leader must not become frustrated with time, but understand God's divine purpose for them being there. Knowing their purpose for being there helps to pinpoint exactly how they want to impact the lives of other students. There are many future leaders right now that are becoming groomed, yet the transition looks rough. Be strong and courageous as Joshua was and don't look to yourself but look to God for help.

The Life of a Leader

Being on campus too long can be frustrating to a leader. Graduation is the only thing on our minds because we are tired of being "professional" students. We have become frustrated with the years we have spent in school to the point where we are just tired of school and want to leave as soon as possible.

When we start college we have our plan mapped on when we want to graduate. However, it seem that God operates on another timetable and will extended your stay for his purposes. It seemed that during my extended season my impact on others and influences became even greater. If you are wondering when you are going to get out of school, or if you are just frustrated with being there, remember God gave each of us the fruit of his Spirit, and one fruit is patience. Knowing this, let "patience have her perfect work" (James 1:4, KJV). If God has prolonged your time in school, it is for a divine purpose. You just haven't recognized it yet. *Time can only reveal the purpose God has for you.*

Though you don't want to be overly involved, you do want to impact lives. I had a chance in college to be a math tutor for three years. This was amazing to me! Here I was, the guy who had taken every math class twice and even three times, yet God used me to be a math tutor to kids who needed me. I tutored at the local high school, and I really had a chance to engage the students and make an impact on their lives. They were going through some of the same frustrations that I had experienced in high school with math as well. I had a chance also to minister and just uplift the name of Jesus and give him credit for my success. I switched from my underclassmen life of being the mentee to now being the mentor.

One of the greatest fears in life can be simply transitioning, leaving one position to go to another. Having to grow up can even be very frightening. It can be frightening because often we don't think we are qualified for where we are being called.

When I look at the life of Joshua, I can see how God prepared him for where he was going even before he got there. Joshua had been a warrior who fought under the leadership of Moses. He was faithful to all that Moses wanted him to do. It was Moses that even gave Joshua his name.

When Joshua stepped on the scene, Moses had just died, and now it was time for him to come into the position. The text reads, "My servant Moses is dead, now therefore arise" (Joshua 1:1, KJV) It is clearly stated the era of Moses was over. Sometimes we hold on to the past. We cling to what we are familiar. Yet now God has called that season to an end and has called us to "arise." We can assume that if you are told to arise, it means that you are not actually at the place you need to be.

Next, God presents not only change, but also a challenge for Joshua. "Go over this Jordan, ye and all this people" (Joshua 1:2, KJV). The goal was to get to the promised land, not to just simply get to Jordan. Sometimes as a new leader on campus, we simply get to the point of being a leader and assume that we have arrived, but there is much more. We have to face some of the same obstacles that our predecessors faced. The great thing about it is that God will be with us the same way he was with them. Being a campus leader and wanting to leave a legacy will be challenging. Yet God has given us the same opportunity as leaders before to make a difference. "As I was with Moses, so I will be with you!" (Joshua 1:5, NIV).

Greatness in Your Name

I once asked a friend of mine what it takes to be well known on campus. He then asked me, "Do you wanna be well known? Or do you want to make a difference?" I thought about it. He continued to tell me that it is possible to be well known but not make a difference. Many people become well known for being the best dressed, cutest girl, having the best personality, or being the funniest, but how many of people can say that they actually made a difference?

One year at a winter dance they were giving out superlatives for our college. As they called off the names, I knew I wasn't going to get any awards for certain categories. They just didn't fit me. Then all of sudden, they called my name. I was surprised. It was for the award of "Most Influential Person." Wow! I was honored. My classmates thought enough to nominate me as being a positive influence in their lives. When I think about my life, I think about Abraham. He started in a normal life as Abram, a shepherd. God then spoke to him in Genesis 12 and told him he was going to have a great name. Even better than that, God said, "I am going to make thy name great," meaning God would provide for him the reputation among people, and he didn't have to make it happen himself.

Jesus was the same way. When he healed many, he would say, "See that you tell no one." He was a man of no reputation. Yet God has given him a name that is above every name.

Are you willing to live college life dedicated to influencing others? Are you willing to go without being recognized in order that Christ be might uplifted? If you are, you will find your name being made great!

Class Notes:

1. Start thinking about the legacy you want to leave behind on campus.

2. Recognize that leadership is challenging and takes transition as well as balance.

3. Remember to give glory to God as he elevates you.

1. Have you gotten frustrated with being in school longer than expected? Why do you think you are still in college?

_____

_____

_____

_____

2. How can you step up into the leadership position or maybe balance out your leadership activities?

_____

_____

_____

_____

3. After you graduate college, how do you want people to remember you?

_____

_____

_____

_____

Prayer for leadership on campus:

Dear God, I know you called us to be representatives of you no matter where we go. You told us to be unashamed of your gospel and to show our light at all times. Let us be that light on the college campus that our friends need to see. We know that our classmates, roommates, and even our teachers are watching to see how we react to life on campus. But more importantly, you are watching us. We don't want to fail you in this assignment. You called us to be more than conquerors. In Jesus's name. Amen.

GRADUATION: THE END OR THE BEGINNING?

Finishing college represents your choice to have faith in God's promises. A spiritual prerequisite for graduation is faith. Understanding the importance of finishing our course can only be realized by faith. Faith will allow you to persevere when you are faced with challenges. When you finish your courses you will not only be accomplishing something for yourself but for those who follow after you. Your testimony will be full of gratefulness because you would have to know that it was God who got you through college.

Knowing God's Promise

"I'm giving you every square inch of the land you set your foot on"(Joshua 1:3, MSG). I recited the scripture quietly as I walked around the buildings on campus not caring about who might hear. Nevertheless, the more I recited it, the louder I got. I began touching the buildings and speaking with boldness concerning the authority in my life on campus. I marched for a few hours as if I was leading a troop of college believers who wanted the same assurance that I wanted, the assurance that God would be with them through the good and the bad times on campus. I was a radical "Jesus freak" that night, and I didn't care. I may have been a freshman at that time, but I wasn't a freshman in my faith.

You may have majored in a number of things, but you can't afford to minor in your faith. Any course catalog will outline for you the number of credits that you need to graduate. Some even map out a plan for you to graduate within a certain time. Many identify the prerequisites to graduate. For believers it is faith. "Now faith is the substance of things hoped for and the evidence of things not seen" (Hebrews 11:1, KJV). If graduating from college is not one of the most "unseen" things, then I don't know what is. You need God's promise to keep away the moments of fear and anxiety.

God reassures us of his promises in times that we are afraid. Being in a new place or position is never easy. Think of how hard it was for Joshua to fill Moses's sandals. Here is Moses, the man who led Israel out of bondage, helped them get across the Red Sea, and even brought them the Ten Commandments. I am sure Joshua had to be a little nervous. Why else would God say, "Be strong and very courageous"? (Joshua 1:6 NIV). Yet, God spoke and reassured him, "As I was with Moses, so I will be with you." So the same God that helped them through the plagues, the Red Sea, and fed them in the desert was now going to do the same for Joshua. That's assurance!

Assurance bring the confidence you need to overcome obstacles. "Being confident of this very thing, that he which hath begun a good work in you will perform it until the day of Jesus Christ" (Philippians 1:6, NIV). So every time I would run into a new issue on campus, I would just remember his promise. When I didn't have enough money for school, I remembered his promise. Bad grade on a test? I remembered his promise. Not enough credits to graduate? I remembered his promise.

"This I recall to mind, therefore I have hope" (Lamentations 3:21, KJV). Knowing God's promises gave me hope for my future. I could see myself dressed in my black cap and gown, stopping to pose for the pictures every few steps as my family and friends surrounded me, blinded by the flashes as I marched across stage, shouting like David! I was so sure about my graduation that I saw my college challenges as mere details to my story. I had pictured my graduation so many times. It was like the preview for an anticipated movie, ending with the phrase "Coming Soon." Finishing was not only important to me, but I know that it brought glory to God as well.

Importance of Finishing

God gets glory when you finish. Understanding the importance of finishing helps the journey. I am not finishing for me. I am finishing for him. "I have brought you glory on earth by completing the work you gave me to do" (John 17:4, NIV). Jesus pointed to God every chance he got. He wanted to let us know that in order to focus, it can't only be about you.

When Jesus came into the world his mission was not to save himself but to save our sinful souls. What if Jesus had only been concerned about himself? He would have bypassed all the suffering and joined his Father in heaven. Yet, he loved us so much that he put on our concerns before his. "My Father, if it is not possible for this cup to be taken away unless I drink it, may your will be done" (Matthew 26:42, NIV). Jesus's future was determined before it began. "And you shall have a son named Jesus and he shall save his people from their sins" (Matthew 1:21, KJV). We all have a purpose to fulfill. Being on the campus, you have a purpose to fulfill, and God knew it even before you were born.

Finishing any goal that you have had is an accomplishment in and of itself. Lots of people have half-finished degrees, one or two semesters short of graduating. Some are just not willing to go back and finish. Despite how talented and gifted people are, frustration kills hope. Some get the college disease called "senioritis." Though I had heard of it while in high school, I never really got it until college. *Was it contagious? What was the cure? Could I go to student services and get a pill for it?* No one warned me of the symptoms of "senioritis." So when my senior year came and I began sleeping late, skipping class, daydreaming, turning in late assignments, and stopped caring as much, I didn't know what was going on. I envision myself at the student health center. "You don't have a fever. Pulse is normal. Oh, I see, from your chart it says that you are a senior this year. That's it!"

There is no better feeling than when you finish with your final exams. A sigh of relief comes over you. After cramming endless hours, you are done. You are acquainted that with great feeling of finishing, yet there are obstacles that stand in the way.

Obstacles in the Way of Finishing

You must decide to overcome obstacles in order to finish your God-given goal. When Nehemiah was leading the people to rebuild the walls of Jerusalem. He faced all types of pressure. He was picked on and ridiculed. People said that he would never finish. They even claimed that if he did finish, the walls wouldn't last very long. There will be plenty of people who will not be in your corner when it comes to graduating. Some will tell you that you won't pass every class. Others will say that your grades are too low to get a job after graduation. Don't give up. Don't let them make you forfeit your blessing. There will be people in your life like those who attacked Nehemiah. They tried to make him lose focus and "to frustrate his purpose" (Nehemiah 4:5, KJV).

He didn't lose focus because he knew how important it was for God's people. Do you really know how important it is for you to graduate? Not just for yourself, but for your family? For some young girl/boy at your church that looks up to you? It is important that you ignore the haters, climb the wall of academics, and graduate. Your finishing will make you a vessel to share your testimony with others who need it.

Share Your Testimony of Finishing

Each semester I had the opportunity to attend graduation. I would stand in the balcony and watch my classmates walk across the stage, the walk that branched from the college world to real life. It was a bittersweet moment for me. If I could make everyone of my friends stay behind in college, I would. I still wish we had more time for more memories. As they would call their names, I would reflect on the stories behind the degree. Each of them had their own personal story of success, tragedy, financial hardships, and frustration. It is amazing how at graduation no one gets to tell their story. Yeah, I know it would be a pretty long ceremony, yet I think a testimony should be squeezed in every now and again. People see your smile, your wave, and possibly your dance or stroll across the stage. Yet only those who are closest to you know the real story. Knowing your story for yourself is so important. "And they overcame him by the blood of the Lamb and by the word of their testimony" (Revelation 12:11, NIV). No other person can tell your story like you can. You have experienced all the ups and downs of college life. Knowing your story is not enough, but sharing your story is important. Where would we be today if the disciples simply knew about the life of Jesus but did not share the life of our savior?

Your story has nothing to do with credits, nothing to do with skill, and shouldn't have anything to do with how smart you were. Your story should point to God—a story of hope. Anyone that talks to you should see God in your story. There were plenty of times I wanted to drop out of school. It would have been easy if I was only thinking of myself. However, it wasn't just about me. It was about those who were coming after me. I wanted to be an example of how God could bless a college student like me who definitely didn't deserve it. Sugarcoating a story would have never gotten anyone anywhere. College students need to be in the "me too" ministry. When I was struggling in college with grades, sex, parties, and a million other issues, all I wanted to hear was another believer say "me too." I just wanted to talk to someone who was real enough to share their heart with me. Therefore, be willing to share your heart.

Christ did not condemn us for our imperfections. He encouraged us to strive for excellence in life. "I am come that you might have life and have it more abundantly" (John 10:10, KJV). That's all I wanted to do. I wanted to finish my story, only to tell it to someone else who needed to hear it. Just like I am writing this book by opening up about my life in college, I hope you will share your story with someone else. Don't run out of college and forget the Lord who brought you through it.

Esther didn't forget. She was beautiful, and she was a Jewish girl who was selected by King Xerxes to be his queen. She had received favor over the other women at the time. After hearing the Jewish people were on the brink of being killed under the order of Haman, her cousin Mordecai urged her with this statement.

> Do not think that because you are in the king's house you alone of all the Jews will escape. For if you remain silent at this time, relief and deliverance for the Jews will arise from another place, but you and your father's family will perish. And who knows but that you have come to royal position for such a time as this?
>
> Esther 4:13-14 (NIV)

To this day, those words ring in my ears. Don't think just because you made it into the corporate America that you are free from temptations of the world. There is still a lot out there in the world. If you decide to keep quiet about your college testimony and not share your story, the great news is that God will get someone else to do it. The bad news is that you would have missed the opportunity. God is trying to get you to share your story with boldness. Don't miss this moment. Briefly below write out one significant experience that happened in your college life.

Class Notes:

1. Remember to know and recite God's promises over your life.

2. Finishing brings glory to God.

3. Obstacles will come your way to the finish, but remember his promises.

1. Share your testimony with someone so that they too can finish the race.

_____

_____

_____

_____

_____

_____

Is there anyone right now by whom you are intimidated when it comes to success?

    1.

    2.

    3.

How will you define success after graduating, now that you won't have grades?

_____

_____

_____

_____

2. Name three reasons you want to finish college (not including anything that has to do with jobs, money, or material gain).

1.

2.

3.

3. Create a list of people you desire to pray for who may be frustrated or have not finished.

_____

_____

_____

_____

_____

_____

Prayer for those who may be struggling to graduate:

Lord God, I thank you for sending challenges in our lives, only to show us that you are strong and mighty. God, many of us have not finished the purpose and the assignment in life that you have given, yet you are still faithful to us even when we are unfaithful. Help us to have the faith to overcome any challenge that may be keeping us from glorifying you by finishing college. It may be social, financial, or personal issues. We know that you are sovereign enough to handle any issue that we may have. Handle it for us, God. Give that student the encouragement to enroll back into school and finish the desire that you have placed within their hearts. In Jesus's name. Amen.

Prayer for those who are at a crossroads in life: Lord, at this crossroad in my life, I am very confused. However, I know that the spirit of confusion did not come from you. Please lead me in a plain path. Guide me to where you would want me to go from here. I need your direction in order that I understand my purpose. Help me to choose the right career to give you glory and to lift up the kingdom of God. In Jesus's name. Amen.

A COLLEGE
SINNER'S PRAYER

I didn't want to take for granted that everyone who read this book knew Jesus Christ as their personal Lord and Savior. Neither did I want you to walk away from this book with only good principles in college, yet not have true eternal life with him well after. Even though this book is for college students, this prayer is for those who may have never let Jesus Christ in their hearts.

> Dear God,
> I haven't been the best these years in school or in my life. I acknowledge that I have sin. I believe that your only begotten Son, Jesus Christ, shed his blood on the cross, died for my sins, and rose again on the third day. I am truly sorry for the things that I have done to offend you. I repent (turn away from my sins). Have mercy on me, cleanse me, and forgive me of my sins as I forgive anyone who has every sinned against me.
> I receive now your free gift of salvation, which was not earned by good deeds or works, but by

what your Son Jesus did on the cross for me. Thank you for coming into my heart and saving me. I now acknowledge you as Lord and Savior over my life. I will now live to please you and not myself. You have my heart, my mind, and my soul from this point on. You said that if any man be in Christ, he is a new creature. Old things are passed away and behold all things are new. My past will no longer hinder me from moving forward to the destiny you have for me. Thank you, Lord, for saving me and making me new in You.

BIBLIOGRAPHY

1. Budziszewski, J. *How to Stay Christian in College.* Colorado Spring: NavPress, 2004. N. pag. Print.

2. Smith, Abbie. *Can You Keep Your Faith in College?* Colorado Springs: Multnomah, 2006. N. pag. Print.

3. Buseck, Craig V. *Seven Keys to Hearing God's Voice.* Tulsa: Hensely Publishing, 2003. N. pag. Print.

4. Harris, Joshua. *I Kissed Dating Goodbye.* Colorado Springs: Multnomah, 1997. N. pag. Print.

5. Life Connections. *Authentic Relationships: Being Real in an Artificial World.* Nashville: Serendepity House, 2003. N. pag. Print

WORKSHOPS/
SEMINARS

If you would like to have the *Jesus Goes to College* workshop come to your church, campus, high school, or community center, then please contact me at

www.JesusGoesToCollege.com

listen|imagine|view|experience

AUDIO BOOK DOWNLOAD INCLUDED WITH THIS BOOK!

In your hands you hold a complete digital entertainment package. In addition to the paper version, you receive a free download of the audio version of this book. Simply use the code listed below when visiting our website. Once downloaded to your computer, you can listen to the book through your computer's speakers, burn it to an audio CD or save the file to your portable music device (such as Apple's popular iPod) and listen on the go!

How to get your free audio book digital download:

1. Visit www.tatepublishing.com and click on the e|LIVE logo on the home page.
2. Enter the following coupon code:
   bc4b-3172-88e3-1497-2f6c-e8f3-d469-8f77
3. Download the audio book from your e|LIVE digital locker and begin enjoying your new digital entertainment package today!